Crosscurrents / MODERN CRITIQUES

Harry T. Moore, *General Editor*

EDMUND WILSON

Leonard Kriegel

WITH A PREFACE BY

Harry T. Moore

SOUTHERN ILLINOIS UNIVERSITY PRESS
Carbondale and Edwardsville

FEFFER & SIMONS, INC.
London and Amsterdam

To Henry Bamford Parkes and Oscar Cargill

Printed in the United States of America
Designed by Andor Braun
International Standard Book Number 0-8093-0523-2
Library of Congress Catalog Card Number 74-156783

Contents

Preface

Leonard Kriegel begins this illuminating book on Edmund Wilson—and it is an illuminating book indeed—by stating the familiar judgment that Wilson is America's "foremost man of letters" of our time. Wilson has of course written widely, but he is primarily a critic; and I'd go along with those who think him the foremost literary critic of the time. The English writer Frank Kermode, whom Mr. Kriegel quotes toward the end of the present book, has said that Wilson has worked at "the legitimate and exhausting tasks of criticism . . . as no other critic in his time." Mr. Kriegel also quotes, with additions of his own, another leading critic when he says, "Having served, in Alfred Kazin's phrase, as 'the conscience of two literary generations,' Wilson has been, almost unnoticeably, metamorphosed into the father of a third and of a fourth." Then there is Frank Kermode's further statement, which called Wilson "the greatest periodical critic of his time," another just observation which in one sense is all too lamentably true.

It is lamentably true because it reveals Wilson's great limitation: that he has not written more books just as books. Wilson has somewhere explained his method, which a good many other critics follow, of first reviewing a literary work and then expanding the review into an article and, finally, rewriting the article somewhat for inclusion in a volume of essays. Too often, however, this works against unity, so that many of Wilson's books are miscellaneous.

This is, as Mr. Kriegel indicates, among much else, true in the case of one of Wilson's volumes which is not made up of literary criticism: his book on our Civil War, called Patriotic Gore. When that volume came out several years ago, I went to New York as one of the National Book Awards judges, after reading about fifty nonfiction volumes under consideration. The other two members on that particular panel were the well-rounded science editor of the New York Times, William L. Lawrence (the only journalist privileged to attend the first atomic-bomb test in New Mexico), and Walter Lord, author of A Night to Remember and other highly readable books on recent history. He naturally enough put up a battle for Barbara Tuchman's The Guns of August, but on the final ballot the other two of us put through the second and third volumes of Leon Edel's biography of Henry James, which a few weeks later was to win the Pulitzer Prize in that category. We had ruled out Patriotic Gore in our judges' discussions of the National Book Awards nominations because it was rather shapeless, a hodge-podge of various articles, however interesting and brilliant each of them was in itself. Afterward, in an elevator of the hotel in which our meetings were held, I met one of the editors of a critical journal, a woman who turned a violently bitter face toward me and hissed, "Why didn't you vote for Edmund Wilson? He's the greatest writer in America!" I said we weren't voting along those lines, but were trying to find the best book of the preceding year. To use the word bitter in a connection with an editor of that particular journal is perhaps redundant, since the magazine, which I gave up reading long ago, prints mainly the contributions of a cabal, most of whose members seem to have had unhappy childhoods.

As noted earlier, some of Edmund Wilson's books besides Patriotic Gore have the scissors-and-paste atmosphere, though it must be admitted that almost everything he writes is brilliant. Impressively enough, early in his life (especially during his Princeton years) he learned Greek, Latin, French, and Italian well enough to read the classics in those languages in the original. In the 1930s, when he was going to visit the Soviet Union, he learned Russian, and in the 1950s, when he was preparing to write on the Dead Sea Scrolls, he studied Hebrew. And then, almost miraculously, in the 1960s he took up the extremely difficult Hungarian language before going on a visit to Budapest and Debrecen, and sufficiently mastered that tongue to be able to understand what was said on the Budapest stage. To many people, these accomplishments would of course be deadening, but not to Edmund Wilson; that activity sharpened and deepened his writings. But what we all miss is a series of more cohesive books. Axel's Castle (1931) and The American Jitters (1932) come closest to that ideal, and incidentally they are the two Wilson books Mr. Kriegel thinks are the best ordered.

Mr. Kriegel throughout is stringently critical of a man whose work he has long admired, as the present volume demonstrates; his admiration shows through, and his criticism is reasonable enough. Edmund Wilson can make mistakes, as he did when he was writing his causeries for the New Yorker just after the Second World War and judged Kay Boyle by one of her lesser novels—a piece he reprinted in a book without exploring Kay Boyle's other work, which has been unduly neglected. There are several other instances of such a tendency in Wilson. Occasionally, however, he usefully goes after the authors of bestsellers, as he did with his essays on Lloyd C. Douglas and Louis Bromfield (are they still remembered?); this is the kind of necessary clean-up job a critic has to do once in a while, and Wilson manages in such cases not to be personally insulting in the manner of a recent English school which has degraded and brutalized the art of criticism. Wilson has expressed a lack of interest in this school because he believes that literary opinions should not be a life-and-death matter. And one might add that in controversy Wilson is an embodiment of Cardinal Newman's definition of a gentleman.

Edmund Wilson's best criticism is something to be

thankful for, as Mr. Kriegel generously shows us. Wilson is at one level a synoptic critic, invariably giving an account of the book on which he is undertaking to comment; and his synopses become in themselves an important form of criticism since his résumés present certain elements in certain books in a certain way. But this is usually only the beginning of a Wilsonian critique, for after he has established what he thinks worth talking about in a novel, play, or poem, he then applies his critical analysis, so often right that he has given some of the finest of all interpretations of literary material, past and present. Mr. Kriegel's judgments of Wilson in this excellent book are all the more valid for being sharply critical; Wilson's good points stand out all the more clearly and define his stature, which among modern critics is one of magnitude.

HARRY T. MOORE

Southern Illinois University
February 12, 1971

Acknowledgments

I should like to thank the City University of New York for a research grant which permitted me to work on this book. I am grateful to the New York Public Library for permitting me to use the Frederick Lewis Allen Room, a home away from home. I have benefitted from conversations with many friends and colleagues, in particular Earl Rovit, Arthur Zeiger, Leo Hamalian, and Theodore Gross. Since 1961, my students at the City College of New York have demonstrated an intellectual independence and critical integrity which, far more than they could have known, has served at least one of their elders as a meaningful model. My greatest single debt is to my wife, for reasons too numerous to list here.

Edmund Wilson

1

"On This Site Will Be Erected"

> *But our American grandeur and dimness are neither allegorical nor elegant: they are natural, almost homely. They are simply a place where people live and where they live a great way apart.*
>
> From *Variations on a Landscape*

This is a book about the work of "the foremost man of letters" in the United States today. Now that it is finished, I can see that it is a mixed tribute. But I should like to believe that it is the kind of book Edmund Wilson himself would find acceptable, for it was *The Shores of Light*, which I read when I was nineteen, that first revealed to me the possibilities inherent in honest reviewing and criticism. I have tried to approach Wilson's work with that same kind of honesty and individuality.

Because this had to be a short study of a prolific writer, I chose to restrict my comments to Wilson's criticism and reviewing, his political journalism and historical essays, his autobiographical writing, and those of his books in which he records his travels. While I have also dealt with *I Thought of Daisy* and *Memoirs of Hecate County*, I have dealt very cursorily, if at all, with his plays, those dialogues he published as "discordant encounters," and his poetry. Like a culture, a writer should stand upon what he does best. If Wilson had written nothing but his plays, his poems, and his dialogues, there would be little interest in his work. This book should then certainly not have been written. For the study of literature remains the study of what is best.

Once the practice of literary criticism had evolved into what R. P. Blackmur termed "a self-sufficient art," it began to suffer from its success. Having become a formal, even institutionalized, aspect of the national culture, it has grown increasingly guilty of taking itself too seriously. So much of the literary criticism one reads is solemn, pompous, even defensive, as if our critics did not truly believe what they were telling each other and the rest of the world. All too often, criticism seems a rather sterile intellectual exercise with no more than a peripheral relationship to the world out of which the poet or novelist must create structure, meaning, and vitality. The dilemma of modern literary criticism is that, increasingly, critics write for other critics. To this, Edmund Wilson has always been an exception: whatever else may be said of him, Wilson has never written primarily for other critics.

One thinks of Wilson as a writer whose appeal is, like the appeal of some nineteenth-century novelist, ultimately personal. If he is to be called a critic, then he is the only critic who seems to deserve the attention we accord Faulkner, Hemingway, and Fitzgerald. Although he is still hailed as our representative intellectual, he seems to be in the process of being absorbed by the institutional aspects of our culture. And where Faulkner, Hemingway, and Fitzgerald share the stature of major creative artists, Wilson is a fugitive from the camp of the creative artist, a writer who probably would have preferred a different influence than the one fate has offered him. But it remains difficult to make much of a case for Wilson as a writer of fiction. At times, *Memoirs of Hecate County* speaks of a strong and directed talent, and *I Thought of Daisy*, despite its burdensome Proustianism, remains the definitive portrait of Greenwich Village in the twenties. But even these novels owe much of their success to Wilson's reportorial skill and to pretend that Wilson possesses significant talent as a novelist is simply not accurate. Like George Orwell, whom he resembles in other respects as well, Wilson is at home in narrative writing only when he can shape the materials of his own life. His autobiographical essays are among his most interesting work; they impart to us a sense of the man as well as of the time. The portrait of Edna St. Vincent Millay which serves as the epilogue to *The Shores of Light* describes a woman who is far more real than the Rita Cavanaugh of *I Thought of Daisy,* and Wilson's own father, obsessed with his integrity and alienated from his time, is drawn far more memorably than the equally obsessed Asa Stryker of "The Man Who Shot Snapping Turtles."

Wilson's desire to be something other than a critic is evident from the beginning of his career. His first book, *The Undertaker's Garland,* was a volume of verse published in 1922 to which Wilson's contributions are decidedly inferior to those of his coauthor and friend, John Peale Bishop. His second book, *Discordant Encounters,* contains some sprightly and entertaining dialogues and one rather poor play. This was followed by *I Thought of Daisy,* which, in turn, was followed by another volume of undistinguished verse, *Poets, Farewell!* It was not until the publication of *Axel's Castle* in 1931 that Wilson presented the literary world with a sustained critical performance. He was then thirty-six years old.

Throughout the twenties, however, he had been demonstrating his ability as a journalist and critic in the pages of *Vanity Fair* and the *New Republic.* To his role as observor of the country and its culture, Wilson brought an incisive mind, a vigorous curiosity, as well as the ability to penetrate to the core of a problem without getting stranded somewhere on its peripheries. Such qualities made him a figure with few peers in American literary history. He functioned within the society as one senses Bourne might have functioned had he lived longer, a writer for whom the critical intelligence, in order to define its own boundaries, must probe the cultural outline of the country. Wilson's particular fusion of intelligence and lucidity is something we have had far too little of in the United States. For nearly half a century, his mind has weighed not only a literature but a national culture in the balance. Having focused on how we live, he has forced his readers to focus on what they live for.

For Edmund Wilson, as for so many of his contemporaries, the 1920s ended with the execution of Sacco and Vanzetti. He was later to speak of that execution as the case that, along with the textile strike in Gastonia, North Carolina, in the autumn of 1929, "made liberals lose their bearings." It was certainly the execution of the two Italian anarchists which forced Wilson to analyze what he, as an intellectual, was doing and what a nation such as America had become. Until that event, his life and work seem characteristic of his generation. He was essentially sympathetic to the postwar revolt against the tone and nature of existence in the United States. If he did not follow the path to Paris, he remained an outsider in his own country, trying to equip himself with Menckenian distance from the spectacle of American life, while, at the same time, he embraced both the world of "the higher jazz" and the world of contemporary literature.

Acutely conscious of his own antecedents, Wilson has published a number of autobiographical essays—and, more recently, the first volume of a journal—which tell us something about his life prior to the twenties. Born in Red Bank, New Jersey, on May 8, 1895 he was the only son of a highly successful but extremely neurotic lawyer and a socially ambitious mother. He grew up in the kind of American household which year by year seems more alien to us; it was wealthy enough not to be ostentatious and it possessed a sense of tradition and a belief in continuity.

From 1908 to 1912, Wilson attended the Hill School in Pennsylvania, where he came into contact with several excellent teachers, among them Dr. Alfred Rolfe, a Greek scholar who was to be the subject of a moving essay included in *The Triple Thinkers*. At Hill, he was exposed to disciplined and intensive study, especially of languages. Few American critics have confronted as many different literatures in the original language as has Wilson and it was at Hill that he first began to acquire his mastery of classical and modern languages.

Wilson's contributions to the *Hill School Record* represent standard schoolboy journalism, just as the poems, essays, and stories he was later to contribute to the *Nassau Literary Magazine* are the work of a very bright but still unprofessional young writer, an undergraduate far more cloistered than he believes. But Wilson's Princeton career is a good example of a young man's being sent to the right school at the right time. By 1912, Princeton had already felt the dynamic impact of Woodrow Wilson's tenure as its president, but it was still "that good eighteenth-century Princeton which has always managed to flourish between the pressures of a narrow Presbyterianism and a rich man's suburbanism." At Princeton, Wilson discovered a group of gifted contemporaries. His friendship with F. Scott Fitzgerald, the first to speak of Wilson as a "conscience," began here, as did his friendships with John Peale Bishop and T. K. Whipple. His most fruitful Princeton relationship, however, was with Christian Gauss, another great teacher; it was Gauss who provided the model for Professor Grosbeake in *I Thought of Daisy;* it was Gauss to whom he was to dedicate *Axel's Castle;* and it was Gauss who was the subject for the prologue to *The Shores of Light.* "Christian Gauss as a Teacher of Literature" is as fine a written tribute as any American teacher has ever received. If *The Shores of Light* is what Wilson intended it to be, a chronicle of how he saw the literature of the twenties and thirties, it is interesting to note how that chronicle is presented, with the essay on Gauss as its prologue and the essay on Edna St. Vincent Millay as its epilogue. Gauss was at the center of Wilson's Princeton experience.

By his senior year, Wilson had been elected editor of the *Lit',* a position which helped prepare him for the journalistic career he was to pursue in New York. But Wilson's Princeton experience must be seen in perspective. If his choice of Princeton was dictated by family tradition, his insight into the social system which had created the peculiar mixture of "narrow Presbyterianism" with "rich man's suburbanism" was acute. His loyalties were to Gauss and to his contemporaries, not to some sentimentalized idea of alma mater. Almost twenty years after he left, he described Princeton in "Disloyal Lines to an Alumnus" as a place of "Deep woods, sweet lanes, wide playing fields, smooth ponds,/—Where clean boys train to sell their country's bonds."

After he graduated from Princeton in 1916, Wilson worked for a year as a cub reporter and reviewer for the staid *New York Evening Sun.* He then spent two years as an enlisted man in the Army, most of which time he was in France as a private attached to the Hospital Corps and then, helped by his father's influence, as a sergeant in the Intellignce Corps.

When the war ended, Wilson returned to New York, a city which he then found "liberating and stimulating," where mere "self-advertisement" could make one "a figure of glamor . . . between the Algonquin and Greenwich Village." For the first half of the decade of the twenties, at least, he found American life invigorating and energetic, even while he deplored its philistinism. Whatever else is to be said of the 1920s, one cannot dismiss the sense of newness, of steady expectancy, that erupted in the United States after the war's end. The fulcrum of that newness was the New York to which Wilson returned, with its skyscrapers, its magazines, its theaters, and, above all, its young and eager writers and artists. Like other young men intent on literary careers, Wilson soon began publishing his poetry, reviews, short stories, dialogues and sketches in such magazines as the *Liberator, Vanity Fair,* the *Bookman,* the *Dial,* and the *New Republic,* which was soon to employ him as an associate editor and which was to remain his chief place of publication until 1941.

Wilson's work during the first half of the decade reveals a nervous intensity matched by a range of interests which moves from Houdini to Hemingway. The articles on "The Progress of Psychoanalysis" and "The People Against Dorothy Perkins, like the articles on art, night clubs, motion pictures, and "The Problem of the Higher Jazz," possess for the contemporary reader remarkable freshness and vitality, as well as a sense of involvement in this world. Wilson's early journalism is even more interesting than his early criticism; he seems to have more room in which to move when he is not primarily concerned with someone else's writing but is rather projecting himself into a dramatic situation. "The People Against Dorothy Perkins," for instance, remains an excellent piece of trial reporting; it manages to maintain the tension of good drama. Even when we read it more than forty years after the event it records, Wilson involves us directly in Dorothy Perkins' fate. The piece is characteristic of his journalism in that he succeeds in surrounding the human situation; at no time does he permit himself to become either saccharine or sensational. The dramatic elements play themselves out before our eyes, but never are they made subordinate to Wilson's thesis. Strangely enough, this was exactly what Wilson was unable to do in the drama itself. Almost all of his plays suffer from didacticism—their terror is rarely the terror of the human. In none of his plays do we sense a real empathy with people, but in his journalism we are almost always aware of this—at least in the journalism written before 1945. In his plays, his characters border on caricature, but in his reporting what is most striking is his ability to project the human. It was this ability, combined with his anger at the pervading economic and social injustice of American life during the early stages of the depression, that was to serve him so well when he came to the social drama we find in *The American Jitters.*

In 1943, Wilson referred to the collected body of his work as "the record of a journalist." From the beginning, his conception of his intellectual role had more in common with the writing of H. L. Mencken than it did with the more analytical criticism practiced by R. P. Blackmur or Kenneth Burke or the intensely moral criticism which was once the domain of the New Humanists and which, with some modification, was carried on in the criticism of Yvor Winters. This is not to say that Wilson's work is not rooted in an energetic moral vision. He possesses a very firm idea of what the world should be and, as he has grown older, he has even approached the position of the New Humanists he once castigated. In some of his work during the past twenty years, he seems a lineal descendent of Paul Elmer More and Irving Babbitt, a rather curious evolution when one recalls his vigorous attacks upon Babbitt and More in the pages of the *New Republic* in 1930. What one sees today is that Wilson's argument was never with morally committed criticism but rather with a criticism predicated upon what he considered a false morality. Until the Second World War, Wilson found the spectrum of modern thought exciting for exactly those reasons Babbit and More found it so depressing: he welcomed its conceptions of new relations, such as those between the organic and inorganic worlds, in the hope that upon such conceptions man could build a new, more substantial, basis for morality. Even *Axel's Castle* is the work of a moralist, its tone consistent with Wilson's desire to replace an increasingly narrow belletristic tradition with the best that industrialism and democratic society had to offer.

American journalists have not been noted for the lucidity of their thought. But Wilson brought to journalism those same qualities which he brought to criticism, a temperament which combined the diligence of the scholar with the curiousity of the novelist. His interests were broader than those of any other American Journalist, including Mencken. And he was not afflicted with Mencken's cultural astigmatism. Until the fifties, his interests were perpetually evolving, and his intellectual range was wider than Mencken's even in the early twenties. Wilson's change in attitude toward Mencken himself offers us a good example of a pupil outgrowing a teacher. At Hill, Mencken, along with Shaw, had been among his chief literary idols. He saw both as "prophets of new eras in their national cultures" and both strongly influenced his journalistic and critical standards. In 1921, he called Mencken "the civilized consciousness of modern America, its learning, its intelligence and its taste, realizing the grossness of its manners and mind and crying out in horror and chagrin." Mencken even seems to have been the mentor for Wilson's style. Not that Wilson was ever as bombastic as was Mencken (nor, perhaps, ever as entertaining); still, one finds in his work that same belligerent forthright approach that one finds in Mencken. Compare the following two sentences, the first from Mencken's essay on Dreiser, written in 1917, the second from a review of Ezra Pound's poems which Wilson wrote five years later:

> The truth about Dreiser is that he is still in the transition stage between Christian endeavor and Civilization, between Warsaw, Indiana, and the Socratic grove, between being a good American and being a free man, and so he sometimes vacillates perilously between a moral sentimentalism and a somewhat extravagant revolt.

> The truth about Ezra Pound is no doubt, as I have already suggested, that he merely presents a new instance of the now familiar dilemma of the clever and sensitive man in the United States of his day: his case has something in common with that of Henry James.

The tone of critical certainty, the a priori assumption of the validity of one's judgment, the lecture-hall approach to an audience to whom one is going to reveal "the truth"—each writer is a cultural judge rather than an explicator.

But the Mencken upon whom Wilson modeled himself was the early Mencken, who had written on Shaw and Nietszche when they had been virtually unknown in the United States and who had directed his invective against middle-class smugness, not the Mencken who took such delight in his role of prophet in the wilderness of Philistine America or the Mencken who emerged, as the 1920s progressed, as merely another bas-relief for college sophomores, to be placed reverently in his niche between Babe Ruth and Rudolf Valentino. By the end of the twenties, Wilson had become far more cautious about Mencken's status as the "civilized consciousness of modern America." The Mencken who wrote *Notes on Democracy* remained a fine stylist, but Wilson had grown as disturbed by the potential effects of the "heavy-footed superman" as he was of the by-now conventional "boob."

Years later, as he surveyed the 1920s, Wilson described the latter half of the decade as a time when a "nervous dissatisfaction and apprehension had begun to manifest itself in American intellectual life." American writers had managed to exist on the vigor of life after the war, but as the decade wore on they came increasingly to desire identification with values and goals more meaningful than energy alone, some affirmative experience that called for discipline and sacrifice and offered them, in return, belief and hope. By 1927, it was already apparent that writers and intellectuals were part of a nation whose energy was beginning to flag, and that they were, like many others in the United States, becoming tired, skeptical, and in danger of drifting. As energy alone proved insufficient, the decade's energies diminished. By 1927, the Dynamo needed more than fuel; it needed to mate with the Virgin. But neither the Dynamo nor the Virgin recognized each other's existence. And so, even before the crash of October 1929, there was a depletion in the decade's literary productivity. Dullness, exhaustion, and doubt characterize the attitude of the nation's writers by the end of the twenties. From his window in New York, Wilson watched while the official order pandered the nation's wealth to business and industry, watched while the national government identified the people's welfare with the welfare of a single class and substituted the interests of wealth and power for the interests of the population-at-large. In the year or two before the depression began, the tone of his writing grows increasingly irritable, a mixture of fatigue, despair, and diminished expectancy.

By 1927, Wilson was already respected—a critic to whom writers paid attention, a journalist who commanded admiration. He was a member of an intellectual community which offered him contact with many of the truly creative people in America. The difficulty for his generation, the root of that "nervous dissatisfaction and apprehension" he later wrote about, was that creativity itself had become less and less sustaining. The execution of Sacco and Vanzetti was not a cause of the intellectual unrest that seized writers and artists; it merely crystallized their sense of inadequacy and purposelessness. Having embalmed Mencken's Puritans on the streets of Greenwich Village and Paris, having buried the Philistines beneath satire and scorn, they could now claim to be as free as their creativity permitted them to be. Unfortunately, it seemed a freedom without responsibility in a culture apparently so valueless that it was stifling. And if they looked at themselves, writers were forced to acknowledge that they had been as much a part of the crudity of American life as any other group in the country. To have spent the decade laughing at that life did not permit one to avoid the fact that the writer was as representative of the tone of that life as the stockbrokers and salesmen he scorned.

Both by nature and heritage, Wilson was alienated from the interests, values, and goals of the American business community. In the twenties, that community dominated American national life. If the business of America was business, then the writer was thrust upon his creative resources as they existed in opposition to the country's life. And as the new ceased to entertain and to satisfy, a writer like Wilson grew bored with the prospect of living in a perpetual party. His struggle to maintain his professional distance, not to permit the chaos to enmesh him, is beneath the surface of what he writes. By 1925, the noise and energy created by the building boom in New York no longer seem fresh; instead, they produce a note of controlled blandness. "One goes on with whatever one is doing, incurious and wholly indifferent." The 1920s were a decade in which the writer's belief in the restorative power of art, a belief so eloquently voiced by Van Wyck Brooks in *America's Coming-of-Age,* was seriously challenged by a culture which simply had no use for what art represented. Babbitt was more than an object of ridicule—he was the American. And while he might have seemed funny in 1922, he had become more and more repressive in his reality. The business culture and the intellectual not only distrusted each other, they lived in worlds which were simply incapable of recognizing each other's existence. For Wilson, this recognition became appalling as the intellectual life alone provided him with less and less sustenance. Both *I Thought of Daisy* and *Axel's Castle* express Wilson's dissatisfaction with that life.

I Thought of Daisy is a period piece. It maintains its charm for us today—it is probably the only one of Wilson's books that one can call charming—because of the fundamental innocence of its characters. *I Thought of Daisy* belongs to the decade of the twenties, to the extent that it is difficult to conceive of a similar novel being written at any other period in our history. When it was reissued in 1953, Wilson wrote a preface to it in which he deplored the novel's excessively "schematic" structure, a structure which he then saw as being "sometimes at odds with the story." And the novel does suffer from Wilson's critical consciousness of Joyce and Proust (many of the insights that were to appear in *Axel's Castle* were already appearing in his *New Republic* reviews as early as 1925), as any novel he published in 1929 was bound to do. It possesses, however, the exuberance of its age—better, in fact, than certain novels that may be artistically superior to it manage to do.

Wilson wanted to portray the disillusionment of a young intellectual both with American materialism and the life of the mind, along with his subsequent reconciliation to an America that "no longer inspired either hatred, apprehension, or scorn." It is not, however, a very convincing reconciliation. From the novel's beginning, the narrator has been adrift in a world which is deeply confusing. Dissatisfied with his lot, he is unable to define the exact sources of his dissatisfaction. The figures of Rita Coleman, the Greenwich Village poetess, and Daisy, the chorus girl who embodies American vitality and energy, form the polarities of his existence, and, by extension, of American existence. It is not until the novel's conclusion, when the narrator has entered into a liason with Daisy and through her "made connections with the common life," that he manages to work through to his reconciliation of self and society, of life and art, and begins to claim an existence that is purposeful. It is as if Wilson were telling us, both through the narrator and through Daisy, that the intellectual life by itself is a failure. In fact, there is throughout the novel a characteristically romantic view of "the common life," an oblique condemnation of intellectual pursuits as lacking vitality and manhood and as permitting the individual to forfeit responsibility for his fate by enclosing himself within a series of abstractions. Daisy, as much a symbol of this America as she is a character, evolves into the source of the protagonist's newfound responsibility by the novel's end.

It remains a testimony to the enduring power of American suspicion of intellectuals that a mind as astute as Wilson's could have framed his novel's conflict in such simple, even simplistic, terms. *I Thought of Daisy* was not intended by its author to be what a few years later was called "proletarian literature," but it shares one of the less fortunate consequences of that literature—a glorification of poverty along with a sense of guilt at being both a bourgeoise and an intellectual. One suspects that the mythical syllogism we see here is as old as Western culture: it is certainly endemic to that culture, for one finds it in St. Paul and in Rousseau. In *I Thought of Daisy*, it serves merely as the source of some brittle, artificial dialogue and makes the novel more dated and self-conscious than it would otherwise seem.

But what remains attractive about the novel is its immediacy, its protrayal of the meeting between a puritanically inspired America and Greenwich Village bohemianism. As late as 1960, one could still see young people running through the Village with *I Thought of Daisy* in their hands. And some of its characters, most notably the novelist Hugo Bamman (drawn, for the most part, from John Dos Passos and with a father who must have been modeled upon Wilson's own father) and the metaphysician, Professor Grosbeake, are attractive for the distinct personal qualities with which Wilson manages to endow them. Unfortunately, a certain disruption of the fictional reality from which these lives stem is equally apparent. What can one say, finally, of an America in which the spirit of the chorus girl is the sole spirit that seems to exist? And is it, one wonders, the artists and the intellectuals who are guilty of cheapening the lives of their countrymen? By the time *I Thought of Daisy* was published, the depression was about to make its own judgment on American vitality during the twenties. Like so many other American writers, Wilson greeted that depression as an event cleansing in the very cataclysm it threatened to bring. In one of the most famous of all literary pilgrimages, he himself moved in the direction of Hugo Bamman's communism.

Axel's Castle was published in 1931, two years after *I Thought of Daisy*. But Wilson had been working on it from 1925. The first serious discussion of symbolism as a literary movement produced by an American critic, it remains one of the truly seminal works of twentieth-century literary criticism. It is, as a matter of fact, the kind of book about which every critic dreams, a work capable of standing beside the best of imaginative literature as a classic in its own right.

This is not to deny that some of the book's appeal is by now dated and that a number of its judgments are open to question. It was Malcolm Cowley who first accused Wilson of "merging symbolism as a literary technique and symbolism as a way of life as though they were the same thing," a charge later reechoed by Stanley Edgar Hyman in his famous attack upon Wilson in *The Armed Vision*. One cannot deny a certain confusion of this sort in Wilson's attitudes toward the writers he chose to discuss in *Axel's Castle*. But such confusion must be seen in perspective; one must take into account the times during which Wilson was working on the book. If literature does not exist in a vacuum, then criticism certainly doesn't. The book grew during those years of "nervous dissatisfaction and apprehension." And many of Wilson's reservations about the actual achievements of the symbolists were reinforced during these years.

Wilson obviously did not find the abstraction of Valéry and the depersonalized character studies of Gertrude Stein to be to his liking. Having always distrusted the oblique and the esoteric, especially when they seemed to have been employed only for the benefit of the writer's sense of coterie and initiation, Wilson continued to insist on a literature that was socially as well as aesthetically ordered. It was not Wilson who created Axel; he merely found in Villiers de L'Isle Adam's young dreamer a type which seemed to him characteristic of the distortions symbolism made of itself. And one can argue that it was not the purpose of the symbolists to look upon themselves only as masters of a technique, for the technique itself, as Wilson correctly pointed out, became a kind of approach to life, almost, one is tempted to say, a philosophy of life.

One must, then, try to re-create the conditions under which *Axel's Castle* took shape, for there is a changing world which stands behind the aesthetic and intellectual order about which Wilson is writing. In the sixty years between 1870 and 1930, the years *Axel's Castle* treats, it was not only imaginative literature that changed but the world's economic, social, and political shape. As *Axel's Castle* was being completed, the American world already seemed to have crumbled beneath the first effects of the depression. This simple economic fact lies behind almost all of the judgments that the book contains. It simply will not do to claim that Wilson was unsympathetic to the six writers whom he chose to single out as examples of contemporary literature's attempt to create imaginative order. He had been among the most enthusiastic advocates of the new literary figures who began to make themselves well known to American audiences immediately after the war. As early as 1922, he had written sympathetically of the French symbolists; in that same year, the first year in which he did full-time reviewing for the *New Republic,* he greeted Joyce's *Ulysses* with great enthusiasm; the following year, he welcomed T. S. Eliot's *The Waste Land;* and his enthusiasm for Proust can be seen not only in what he wrote about Proust but in the fact that he chose to attempt a Proustian novel in *I Thought of Daisy.* There are clear and obvious connections between the philosophical bias of a work of criticism and the conditions under which that work is created. While we recognize this where imaginative literature is concerned, we do not seem to accept it for the critic. We still desire a criticism that speaks *sub specie aeternitatis.*

At the center of *Axel's Castle,* implicit in all of the judgments it makes, is the modern writer's dilemma as Wilson then saw it. It is this which forces him to analyze symbolism as something more than a literary technique, for symbolism, even considered as a literary technique, had created certain specificially nonliterary consequences. And if it is true that symbolism as a literary technique and symbolism as a way of life are two different things, then the symbolists themselves were guilty of muddling the issue, since the human contacts of their art had become increasingly fragmented. Literature is something more than a cloister in a circus.

Insofar as symbolism was a technique, *Axel's Castle* was not opposed to symbolism. But what disturbed Wilson was the social isolation which seemed implicit in symbolism and which threatened to change it from a literary movement into an aesthetically precious social and intellectual langueur; what disturbed Wilson was the way in which many of the symbolists, and Valéry is a notable example here, simply refused to look at the world beneath the window. If our servants are to live for us, Wilson asks, taking up Adam's thesis, then what are we to make of their lives, either artistically or socially?

The "solitary labor and . . . earnest introspection" displayed by Valéry are simply not enough, especially when they are contrasted to the strength of Anatole France, a strength which grew out of the writer's awareness of "a wide knowledge of human affairs, a sympathetic interest in human beings, direct contact with public opinion and participation in public life through literature." The absence of passion and of personality which became so characteristic of the symbolic method as it grew had succeeded only in reducing the dimensions of the human. And was Wilson unjustified in condemning Valéry for that poet's expressed distaste for Anatole France because France had failed to champion symbolism? France, after all, had championed an entire tradition, the tradition of intellectual committment which had, until his time, been developed further by the French genius than by the genius of any other people. "France had," Wilson reminds us, "invited popular hatred, had sacrificed his place in the Academy and had embroiled himself with his friends, in defending the innocence of Dreyfus." Wilson creates of the Dreyfus Case something similar to Matthew Arnold's cultural touchstone; and he portrays Valéry as a prisoner of his own dislike of democratic and industrial civilization. In a key both to *Axel's Castle* and to his own critical method, Wilson makes of Valéry's funeral sermon on Anatole France on the occasion of his succeeding to France's chair in the French Academy the dramatic confrontation of two different ideas of what the life of the artist is and what it should be. We are asked to distinguish not merely between the works of these two men, but between the atmosphere, the conditions of creation, the styles of life which brought those works into being. One must frame a literature against a particular background before one can truly claim to know it. And if it is for this that Wilson has been criticized, then the criticism has been futile. Wilson's intention has never been to solve literary acrostics and he has never looked at literature as a "superior amusement." Historical development means as much to him as aesthetic development, and if he tends, at times, to ignore the latter, his critics frequently are oblivious to the former.

Wilson has been excessively criticized in this area, even by those who are sympathetic to the kind of criticism he practices. So astute a mind as F. O. Matthiessen's objected to his treatment of Valéry, Yeats, and Eliot on the grounds that he had failed to give "us rounded estimates of their poetry." But to limit criticism to such estimates, or even to demand them, threatens the very necessity of criticism. It produces those very same "oracular" tendencies which Wilson deplored in the chapter on Eliot in *Axel's Castle*. Anyone who has experienced an undergraduate education in English literature since, say, 1935 can only wince when Wilson describes the unfortunate tendencies inherent in Eliot's critical essays. One wonders, indeed, whether a good deal of the hostility Wilson engenders in certains types of academics cannot untimately be attributed to his refusal to subscribe to the terrible ponderousness of modern literary criticism, armed, as it so frequently is, not only with a "scientific" vocabulary but with a metaphysical teleology. A good part of the chapter on Eliot is devoted to a discussion of contemporary criticism, for much of which Eliot bears a certain responsibility. The detached aura of professionalism when dealing with literature and culture, the theological approach to culture, the disdain for the present, a certain worship of what is obscure and pedantic—all of this, while certainly not peculiar to Eliot alone, has at least received a certain impetus from the kind of criticism Eliot wrote. Eliot's ideal of culture, as Wilson pointed out long before Eliot wrote his *Notes Toward the Definition of Culture* or

> Yeats rejected the methods of Naturalism and applied himself to the introspective plumbing of the mysteries of the individual mind. While Yeats was editing Blake, Shaw was grappling with Marx; and Yeats was appalled by Shaw's hardness and efficiency. "I hated it," he says of "Arms and the Man"; "it seemed to me inorganic, logical straightness and not the crooked road of life and I stood aghast before its energy." And he tells us that Shaw appeared to him in a dream in the form of a sewing machine, "that clicked and shone, but the incredible thing was that the machine smiled, smiled perpetually."

This kind of criticism simply fails to do justice to Yeats, and not only because it measures him at his most questionable against Shaw at his most assured. Yeats might have been "convinced that the world of science and politics was somehow fateful to the poet's vision," but a single poem such as "The Second Coming" speaks far more authoritatively of the prospect before us than does the "logical straightness" of *Arms and the Man.* Shaw might have studied Marx, but Yeats absorbed the peculiar dread of the politics of our century. The instincts that led him to Blake might have been surer than those that led Shaw to Marx. Even Wilson's images do little more than load the dice against Yeats. Like Atlas, Shaw shoulders a world of information and responsibility; Yeats, on the other hand, is a kind of plumber delving into muddied and stagnant waters. By the time he wrote this chapter, Wilson had become so immersed in the democratic-industrial argument that his criticism was the victim of his sympathies. What Wilson was criticizing was Yeats's refusal to accept the mold of socialist consciousness. It is too harsh a demand to make of Yeats, in whose poetry modernism itself promised a return to a more vital past.

But the finest chapters in *Axel's Castle* are those devoted to Proust, to Joyce, and to a summation of Wilson's treatment of symbolism. The chapter on Proust, especially, shows Wilson at his best. It remains one of the finest critical essays Wilson ever wrote. He was attempting here "to give a meaning to our experience," in this case our experience of a novel which indicts an entire civilization. The essay is not only a historical examination of Proust and of the method Proust used in writing his great novel, it is also a moralist's probing of history in terms of the novel. It is the kind of literary criticism which has been practiced more successfully in Europe than in the United States, a criticism in which the critic serves as a social and intellectual historian whose task is to explain why form, too, follows economics and sociology.

Few other critics writing in 1931 were capable of so complete an analysis of the influences that went into Proust's great novel. The pages devoted to Dickens's impact upon Proust go a long way toward enlightening those readers who have already felt how un-French Proust's broad humor is. Wilson is intent not merely on positioning Proust in modern thought and literature, but on the task of making Proust's mind and art available to the reader. When he writes that Proust is "one of the great minds and imaginations of our day, absolutely comparable in our own time . . . to the Nietzsches, the Tolstois, the Wagners and the Ibsens," he has first made sure that we have Proust's achievement available. Elucidation and analysis are followed by judgment, until the debt is ours when the essay concludes with the following magnificent sentence:

> Proust is perhaps the last great historian of the loves, the society, the intelligence, the diplomacy, the literature and the art of the Heartbreak House of capitalist culture; and the little man with the sad appealing voice, the metaphysician's mind, the Saracen's beak, the ill-fitting dress-shirt and the great eyes that seem to see all about him like the many-faceted eyes of a fly, dominates the scene and plays host in the mansion where he is not long to be master.

The chapter on Joyce is one which graduate students are almost invariably told is dated and valueless; it is, in fact, almost the equal of the chapter on Proust, although Wilson was working without the benefit of the full text of *Finnegan's Wake,* only part of which had appeared in *Transition* when *Axel's Castle* appeared. The difficulty, of course, in even reading Wilson on Joyce is that one must try to forget the sheer volume of Joyce scholarship in this country, what the English have recently come to call "the Joyce industry." For all of the talk of its being dated, Wilson's observations about *Ulysses* and *A Portrait of the Artist as a Young Man* are extremely perceptive, for they illuminate both the brilliance and limitations of Joyce's methods. And they are surprisingly refreshing observations, especially after the humorless pomposity of so much Joyce scholarship. How many of us have simply not had the courage to state what we believed about *Ulysses,* that Joyce had, in Wilson's words, "tried to put too many things into it"? And yet Joyce remains, for Wilson, one of the very few writers who has "done justice to all those elements in our lives which we have been in the habit of describing by such names as love, nobility, truth and beauty." Like the essay on Proust, this chapter succeeds in making the art of Joyce more attainable. In this, it performs an invaluable service for the contemporary reader, who is bound to be frightened of any author who has been as incorporated into academic culture as Joyce has. When one has finished the chapter, he understands why Wilson speaks of Joyce as "the great poet of a new phase of human consciousness."

There remains the task of placing the symbolist movement in perspective and of defining its limitations for modern writers, a task which Wilson accepts in the final chapter. We have seen how *Axel's Castle* incorporates the conditions of the times during which it was written, and nowhere is this more in evidence than in "Axel and Rimbaud," which offers us the "two alternative courses" with which the artist can reject modern industrial society. The argument is very persuasive, but one wonders whether Wilson has not overlooked the course followed by a writer such as Mann, who might have offered him a mediating agent between Yeats and Shaw and, in this way, avoided the repudiation of modern life implicit in both Axel and Rimbaud. In any case, Wilson is now intent on taking leave of a literature that exists outside the possibilities of action in his own time. The breakdown in the American economy forced him to embrace what he called "social-idealistic literature." He rejects "Axel's world of the private imagination in isolation from the life of society [which] seems to have been exploited and explored as far as for the present is possible." Nor has the development of literature since 1931 proved him wrong in his diagnosis. The lack of fulfilment of American life appeared permanent, or at least as permanent as American capitalism; the chaos was everywhere apparent. And yet, Wilson, even in rejecting them as possible guides, never rejected the literature which the symbolist writers he had chosen to include in his book had produced, and which, he believed, was "comparable to the work of any time." But the world was changing. The traditional culture seemed to be dying, while

> Americans and Europeans are both becoming more and more conscious of Russia, a country where a central social-political idealism has been able to use and to inspire the artist as well as the engineer. The question begins to press us again as to whether it is possible to make a practical success of human society, and whether, if we continue to fail, a few masterpieces, however profound or noble, will be able to make life worth living even for the few people in a position to enjoy them.

Wilson had made his choice. But he had made it with a characteristically quiet honesty. It had served him well in the twenties; it was to serve him even better as he moved into his years of protest and pain.

2

A "Truly Human" Culture

By rights, he should have been also a Marxist, but some narrow trait of the New England nature seemed to blight socialism, and he tried in vain to make himself a convert.

From *The Education of Henry Adams*

And Bunny, swinging along confidently with his cane toward his cloister in a carnival, has gone over to Communism and frets about the wrongs of southern mill workers and western farmers whose voices, fifteen years ago, would not have penetrated his study walls.

From Fitzgerald's *The Crack-Up*

Wilson has always been a peculiarly American writer, despite the fact that he is, intellectually, a man of the world. Like so many of our writers, he has felt that peculiar sense of disaffiliation that the writer in America feels. American writers are constantly defining both self and work in terms of their relation to the country. That strange mixture of love and hatred is, at its best, absorbed into the writer's desire to create of his own work a part of the landscape. American writers, even when they are most virulent in their attack upon the middle class, are never quite as revolutionary as they would have us believe. They are too Emersonian, and Emerson is not a revolutionary, at least not the kind of revolutionary from whom governments have very much to fear. Christianity's success is proof enough that revolutions of the spirit can be accomodated by conservative governing bodies. Wilson's creeping dissatisfaction with American life produced a growing doubt about national ideals and cultural goals. And it created a questioning of self and class which led him first to Marxism and ultimately to a kind of aristocratic isolation from the tenor and aims of American life. Wilson's desire to "take Communism away from the Communists" can only be understood as the remark of an intellectual who became a victim of history.

As a moralist, Wilson had served an Augustinian apprenticeship. His essays on his family, as well as the first volume of his memoirs, point to a background that was always threatening. In America, the sons of patricians do not generally fare too well, and, by the beginning of the thirties, all that Wilson could bring to the social and political chaos he saw was an idea of serviceable intellect. Critical discovery and self-expression had proved to be inadequate. Perhaps the best picture of what Wilson went through is to be found not in any of his own essays or novels—with all of his brilliance as a writer of autobiographical essays, one senses a certain caution in Wilson's approach to himself—but in the kind of isolation from one's own past depicted by Malcolm Cowley in *Exile's Return*.

What ultimately was to save Wilson from the misanthropy of Mencken or the elitist detachment of Henry Adams, for whom a world without Adamses was a narrow world indeed, was a burgeoning sympathy for the dispossessed, the hungry, the beaten. To fret "about the wrongs of southern mill workers and western farmers" was not, as Fitzgerald thought, a betrayal of literature; it was, rather, an acknowledgment that the writer's subject and the writer's concern were one and the same. It is rather ironic that Wilson has achieved a reputation as a writer who, even in the 1930s, combined an interest in "social conditions . . . with a disinterest in people as individual human beings." Stanley Edgar Hyman is not alone in portraying Wilson as a misanthrope, and if one chooses to focus on isolated remarks in his work during the 1930s support for such a thesis can be found. But it remains a weak case, especially when one considers both the nature and quality of the work he was doing in the thirties. One finds in a book like *The American Jitters* that same kind of compassion for individuals that makes Orwell's *The Road to Wigan Pier* so memorable a document. In his chapter on Wilson in *The Armed Vision*, Hyman suggests that "Wilson has a special insight into the minds and work of disillusioned radicals." The entire chapter is written with a remarkably vindictive animus toward Wilson, but the remark itself is accurate: it is an insight Wilson shares with Silone and Orwell and Koestler and Malraux, and it is created out of a virulent contempt for the way in which modern Marxism turned itself into an apologia for the Soviet Union. What Wilson sought to change in the 1930s was a system which had dispossessed men, which was characterized by economic, social, and political injustice, and which seemed indifferent to the fact that some men went hungry while others destroyed food in the interests of an economic system that ground men down to statistics. As a scholar and as a journalist, the thirties were to be Wilson's most creative decade, the only period in which it could be said that he found a way out of the aimlessness of modern life. If he guessed wrong in his expressed desire to "take Communism away from the Communists," his efforts reflected his attempt to get back to what his mentor on the *New Republic*, Herbert Croly, had called *The Promise of American Life;* Wilson, in fact, wanted to broaden that phrase into "a culture which is above classes and which will be the first culture that is truly human." The words, of course, are Trotsky's, but they speak as well as anything else of why Wilson moved to the Left—and of why he was soon to retreat from that which he was ultimately to view, with the "special insight" of the "disillusioned" radical, as the greatest betrayal in history.

It was not until November 5, 1930, that Wilson's first political article, "Dwight Morrow in New Jersey," appeared in the pages of the *New Republic*. The article marks not only Wilson's first extensive consideration of the depression but, perhaps more important, his entry into political journalism. Until 1937, he wrote more about politics and history than he wrote about literature. What literary criticism he did write during this period took its tone from the effects of the depression. His "Notes on Babbitt and More" indicated his impatience not only with humanism but with the deadening conservativism of the official culture. Later that same year, on November 26, 1930, he published a brief article on the Thorton Wilder-Michael Gold controversy, which, despite the ties of class, education, and friendship which he shared with Wilder, took Gold's side.

The most decisive indication of Wilson's shift in interests came in the last of his *New Republic* articles for 1930, "Foster and Fish." As was so often the case, Wilson was able here to use the very talents he could not seem to command in his role as dramatist. The confrontation between the leader of the American Communist party and the congressional representatives investigating communism in the Unted States is dramatically manipulated in a far more convincing fashion than any single scene one can think of in Wilson's plays. Wilson had discovered the symbolic embodiments of the issues and alternatives at stake in the course the nation would choose in these two men. The physical appearances of Fish and his fellow investigators are effectively contrasted with those of the Communist leaders. Fish's "coarse features, broad shoulders and . . . finicking manner" are organized into the metaphorical "blank-eyed vacuous Bashan bull." Representative Bachman of West Virginia is "the caricaturist's ideal of the lower order of congressmen: he is pot-gutted and greasy-looking, with small black pig-eyes and a long pointed nose." Representative Nelson of Main, the only member of the committee who apparently disapproves of the hearings, is portrayed rather sympathetically as "a portly man with a white waistcoat and a gay red carnation in his buttonhole." The representative from Tennessee is "an old gentleman," who wears an "open congressional collar and a black ante-bellum bow tie" and who possesses antebellum manners. Sitting "with his arms hanging down beside his chair and his mouth gaping open," he embodies the decay that has seized both the Congress and the country whose political purity it seeks to protect.

The Communists, on the other hand, are far more alive, both physically and mentally. If the Fish Committee represents the decay of American capitalism, then the Communists, as Wilson portrays them, represent those forces which can bring a socialist America into being. Foster himself, with "his finely modelled brow and nose" and his "plebian Irish lantern jaw" is the very model of "an American workman with a grievance against his employer, attempting to defend his rights." Israel Amter, who follows Foster to the stand, is one of the earliest of Wilson's messianic Jews, "dark, intense and fine-looking," with "intelligent liquid brown eyes." In Amter, one sees Wilson's growing tendency to identify with the Jews as a group which struggles against all forms of political and social injustice, a tendency later to be reflected in his insistence upon the importance of Marx's Jewish background, in his identification with Trotsky as a supreme figure of alienation, and in his essays on "The Jews" in *A Piece of My Mind* and on "Israel" in *Red, Black, Blond and Olive*, in which his deep appreciation of and affinity for the moral tradition inherent in Judaism are developed.

Both "Dwight Morrow in New Jersey" and "Foster and Fish" were to be incorporated into *The American Jitters*, one of the finest examples of political journalism provided in a decade noted for its political journalism. Wilson's theme is the effect the depression is having upon individuals in America and his approach is essentially dramatic. The approach was to be made into a method in *To the Finland Station*, where history itself is a drama written by historical thinkers and created by historical actors. If as a theory of behavior this is too simple, as a poetic metaphor which embodies an artistic vision of history it is remarkably successful.

What one finds in the writing of "Foster and Fish" is what one finds in virtually every single piece which Wilson wrote for the *New Republic* in 1931—most of which went into *The American Jitters*—the controlled anger and outrage of an artist convinced that society is incapable of humanizing itself without a revolution. In retrospect, one can criticize Wilson for framing the dialectical alternatives so unequivocally. Fish, and what Fish represented, was not a very worthy opponent; it is too easy to agree with Wilson that "in the presence of the Communists today, these members of our government seem lacking either moral force or integrity." Because Wilson chose to cast what were essentially social issues in the form of a dramatic tableau, it seems fair to ask why he did not widen the choice. Roger Baldwin of the American Civil Liberties Union followed Foster and Amter to the witness stand. Both in background and in perspective, Baldwin was far closer to Wilson than either Foster or Fish. Where the Communists have "communism behind them and the congressmen have the American government," Baldwin possesses only his "truculent independence and his tense insistent will." "A furious individualist" who calls himself an anarchist, his life has been devoted to "the defense of free speech." But Baldwin also represents for Wilson a point of view, which, however noble its intention, has nothing very meaningful to offer depression America. What Wilson finds attractive in Foster and Amter is that they possess more than compassion: they possess discipline, conviction, and hope, qualities which he could find nowhere else. If he is conscious of "the awful eye of the Third International" upon them, he is also aware of the irrationality of a dehumanizing capitalism. So irrational is American society that it justifies both Foster's rhetoric and communism's logic. Baldwin stands before the committee in the splendor of his own isolation, a form of permanent exile; his was a road that led deeper and deeper into the burdensome independence of the self. Ultimately, Wilson was to choose a similar course.

But by the end of 1930, Baldwin's road seemed to lead nowhere. Integrity was not enough. What Wilson desired was belief in something beyond one's individual self. And in spite of his professed distaste for religion, he found the church of the Third International attractive. Foster and Amter are "at once the apostles of a religion and the captains of an army." The attraction that communism held, both for Wilson and for other American intellectuals in the early thirties, was anything but illogical. The depression was not the fault of the Communists. It was the fault of the businessmen and the politicians, of the legions of the "fatuous" for whom Wilson felt such contempt. For writers, the depression was "not depressing but stimulating." Nor was the movement to the Left of Wilson and other writers representative of what Murray Kempton described as "an aesthetic rather than a social tendency." Wilson's quarrel with communism was never aesthetic; it was, rather, moral. The promised land was to be overwhelmed by the years in the wilderness.

The very first article Wilson wrote in 1931, "An Appeal to Progressives," showed that he rejoiced in the prospect that the failure of American society was permanent. The piece opens as a tribute to Herbert Croly, who had died eight months earlier. While Wilson pays tribute to the vision that conceived of *The Promise of American Life,* he rejects Croly's refusal to look at American social and economic problems from the vantage point of class. By 1931, Wilson, like John Chamberlain, found reform insufficient. The changes in the social structure which were so necessary could not, the Left intellectuals believed, be provided by further legislation. The political processes of the country were bankrupt. Wilson focused on the inability of most American intellectuals to concede that the spirit of reform was no longer adequate to treat the kind of economic and political disintegration which afflicted the country. Traditionally, reform movements had been constructed around the idea that the nation could work toward a "benevolent and intelligent capitalism" capable of functioning without constricting the development of democratic society. Wilson now called upon his fellow intellectuals to recognize that for as long as American life was dominated by capitalism, "any further spectacular appearance of revival" was nothing "more than a spurt depending on . . . overinflation." The language of economics was still strange to him, but the moral indignation behind his use of that language was not.

The lassitude and apathy which had characterized the nation's reaction to the early stages of the depression was, Wilson believed, a decisive indictment of a society that had little working for it other than "the momentum of money-making." And this momentum, which had become a national ideal, had seized the culture, too; it offended Wilson's patrician instincts. American acquisitiveness was justified through a false sense of what America was. If there had been a certain social value in such old American myths as the settling of the frontier, it was time to recognize that such myths no longer possessed any meaning.

All of this was intended to lead to the question Wilson wished his fellow liberals to answer: what did they intend to do about the country's situation? Although the liberals professed distaste for American acquisitiveness, they had also, through their inability to conceive of alternatives to capitalism, acquiesced to its dominance of the nation's life. The chief reason for the ineffectiveness of liberalism was that it conceived of capitalism as permanent and had been unable to offer any program more daring than "a discreet recommendation of public ownership of water power and certain other public utilities" to change America. Wilson's indictment of liberalism is similar to the indictment of liberalism which the New Left makes today: in working through the system, the liberal inevitably becomes part of it.

Despite their failure, Wilson was convinced that the depression had given liberals their best—and possibly last—chance to alter radically a society designed to support the "fatuous," to destroy, once and for all, the "whole money-making and -spending psychology" which was strangling the more positive aspects of American life. If the country was floundering, then it was the responsibility of liberals not to flounder with it; instead, they would have to act decisively, to break through the lassitude and drabness of a commercial civilization. And the only political idea capable of providing liberals with the ideological support they needed in order to act decisively was Marxism. In order to establish a meaningful culture in an egalitarian society, the liberals would have to "take Communism away from the Communists, and take it without ambiguities, asserting that their ultimate goal is the ownership by the government of the means of production." Foster had not only triumphed over Fish; Wilson was now ready to replace him.

Wilson's movement toward communism was individual, but he was speaking for a significant segment of the American intellectual community. His movement to the Left arose out of his own patrician past—his intellectual discipline, his natural aversion to a society with whose values he could have but little sympathy, and, above all, his growing identification with the dispossessed, the weak, the hungry. Over the past two decades, Wilson has become so completely identified with the rather querulous older man who moves like some literary Buddha between Wellfleet and Talcottville that his affinity with the poor cannot be overstressed. Like Orwell, Wilson's sympathies with the outcasts of this earth had sprung from his art. What pushed him toward communism was, quite simply, human suffering. Intellectually, communism caused him great misgivings even when he was closest to embracing it. Its stringently dogmatic nature was already apparent. The ugly fratricidal struggle that had broken out to determine Lenin's successor had already resulted in Trotsky's exile and in the persecution of his friends and followers; the American Communist party had already been rent by a number of purges which left some well-known victims in their wake; and by 1931, Stalinist dogmatism showed signs of becoming more rather than less rigid. And yet, this was the system Wilson wished to seize in the name of his fellow liberal intellectuals. For him, the choice had quite simply become communism or chaos. The chaos was already apparent; communism was yet to be tried. To believe that it was possible for American liberals to seize control of a party structure they were not even able to understand was undoubtedly naïve. But Wilson chose communism not because of but despite "the awful eye of the Third International." At the beginning of 1931, his "Appeal" seemed the only logical plea he could make.

Until this point, Wilson's most distinctive attribute as an intellectual was his essential freedom from cant and dogmatism. As a critic, he had always been concerned with the question, What is this writer telling us? It was, as a matter of fact, because this concern was so central that he had been accused—with some justice—of ignoring a work's artistic form for the sake of its content. And he had remained consistent in refusing to subscribe to any of the various orthodoxies which afflicted so many intellectuals in the twenties. In an essay on Eliot, published in 1929, he examined with dispassionate accuracy the palaces of dogma in which writers as different from one another as Eliot, Mencken, Dos Passos, and Pound had sought refuge from the complexities of modern existence. Mythologies were personal; for Wilson, they were therefore also illusory. He had as little use for Dos Passos's "myth of a serious-minded and clear-eyed proletariat" as he did for Eliot's incense-drenched "aristocratic myth" or Mencken's "German university town where people drink a great deal of beer and devour a great many books." As an intellectual, Wilson was instinctively pragmatic. He was to value systems insofar as they seemed usable and to distrust system-builders insofar as they seemed blind. It is this which lies behind his rather curious attitude toward Marx in *To the Finland Station;* it is obvious that he pits his preference for Engels as an individual against his recognition of Marx as a thinker.

From Wilson's point of view, Croly's promise had negated itself by 1931, for it was a promise which simply had not envisioned a social catastrophe as total as that of the depression. And for those American intellectuals who, like Wilson, felt themselves enmeshed in a culture which they saw as both corrupt and stifling, the depression was, indeed, a welcome relief. It has been fashionable to speak of communism as a church and of Marx as its God the Father. It is certainly time to bury such metaphors, but for the writers who, having come of age during the First World War, were blistered and baked in the twenties, the metaphor was appropriate enough. Hungering for refuge from the flesh and pain of economic reality, many of them became communicants at the altar of the dialectic. For most of them, the conclusion which John Dos Passos voiced in *The Big Money* said all that needed to be said about their country: "All right, we are two nations." Even without the rhetoric of the class struggle, choice was easy enough. Perhaps the chief reason why the depression decade produced more of value in the way of journalism than it produced of value in the way of fiction was that in journalism the writer was able to depict the breakdown of the system as the stuff of human suffering—a task which was far more difficult for the novelist.

The American Jitters, based upon the articles Wilson wrote for the *New Republic* about his travels through the country in 1931, constitutes one of the most impressive portraits of depression America that we have. Perhaps Sherman Paul overstates the case when he calls it "superior" to *The Grapes of Wrath,* but one can claim for it a place alongside Agee's *Let Us Now Praise Famous Men* for the way in which it develops the impact which the communion of suffering had upon one American. It stands at the beginning of the depression very much like Agee's book stands at the end. When read together, they tell us as much as we can actually absorb about what the depression actually did to men and women.

Opening with "Dwight Morrow in New Jersey," the book moves through the geography of American humiliation during the early years of the depression, its tone at once bitter and ironic. Wilson does not permit the reader to look at the depression simply as a breakdown of the economic system. He forces the reader to accompany him through this landscape, in some of the best writing he ever achieved, until the book closes with "The Case of the Author" and its quiet prediction: "So far as I can see, then, Karl Marx's predictions are in process of coming true."

The effect of the book upon Wilson's fellow intellectuals was considerable. John Chamberlain's reaction was representative. As he himself moved Left, Chamberlain applauded this "graph upon which the intellectual pilgrimage of a social critic of real stubborn integrity may be traced through twelve months of heavy pressure." Wilson covered every section of America. His descriptions of the cities and towns he visited are remarkably consistent, each of them stressing the dehumanizing geometry in which an industrial capitalism molds the life of its victims. All richness is artificial, dull, as flat and lifeless as the people at whose expense it has been squeezed out.

Basically, Wilson treats three groups of people: the exploiters and their servants; the exploited and victimized; and the men of new vision, who see the depression, along with Wilson, as an opportunity to create certain fundamental changes in American society. In the first group, we find Henry Ford, overlord of Detroit, and the Reverend Bob Schuler, pastor of Trinity Church and guardian of public faith and morals in the city of Our Lady the Queen of Angels. It is to this class that the imaginary composites, "Mr. and Mrs. X," aspire. Unlike Lincoln Steffens, for whom Ford, like Lenin and

Mussolini, belongs to the mainstream of historical development, Wilson does not excuse Ford's career as the inevitable trimuph of action over thought. We see Ford himself as the end product of the system he tried to create, a man whose every move is blanketed by childish fears and anxieties, a man whose modernity consists of a faith in gadgetry. Ford is more fascinating than the cars his workers produce. The Ford system, characterized by the speedup and the company police, is stupid and inhumane as well as inefficient. Ford himself is "the despot of River Rouge," whose life is "full of suspicions and shrinkings" despite his having surrounded himself with "professional yes-men who live in terror of differing with him." It is Wilson's great virtue as a journalist that he can make the extraordinary something remarkably elementary. And Ford is elementary. The portrait of Ford in "Detroit Motors" is as profound an indictment of the system as the portrait of the disillusioned English mechanic who comes over to America only to discover that "Ye get the wages, but ye sell your soul at Ford's." Detroit, for whose growth Ford bears such responsibility, is as lifeless as American capitalism, a dreary, mechanical city, a monument to an industrialism that seems to have run into the ground. The city seems to swallow the American vision: "On the dreary yellow Michigan waste with its gray stains of frozen water, the old cars wait like horses at the pond."

But Wilson is not searching for a villain. The system needs none. Ford himself is a victim, although Wilson never lets us forget that he is the victim who possesses power. It is the living dead, the beaten workers of Detroit and the "dog-run" people of the Kentucky hills for whom even speech has become almost impossible as they welter in a surreal hell, toward whom Wilson himself strains. Monotony is the key to their lives, and monotony is the key to the dreadful compassion Wilson feels in "Red Cross and County Agent." It is not so much that he pities them; it is, rather, that in their victimization they seem worse than lifeless. Their very physical presence assumes that the system can abide no human values, that the dreariness must ultimately infect even those who try to make life somewhat more tolerable. Existence is the here and now of nothing. Even pity seems a wasted emotion, for the people themselves have been caught in a vise that has simply locked. They are dazed, they are frightened, they are unable to fight back because they simply do not possess the insight to penetrate to the core of what is happening to them. "A Bad Day in Brooklyn" depicts three suicide attempts—one, a young German who had emigrated to the United States in search of independence; the second, a young Jewish housewife, the mother of three children, married to an unfaithful "loafer" who periodically deserts her; the third, a skilled Italian immigrant machinist who has lost his job as shop superintendent of a company on Long Island. None of these people can answer for his own fears, his own loves, his own sense of belonging. The system works in its inexplicable way. And the system is always the system. "A Bad Day in Brooklyn" ends on the following note: "Mrs. Dimicilli says that the Italians who comes to the United States and go in for racketeering have wonderful opportunities, but that it is no place for a skilled machinist."

The journey is rescued from despair by the individuals Wilson meets who give him hope for the future. It is they who wish to change America, to reconstruct the system, to create a wider range of human possibilities. They come from different backgrounds and they occupy different positions, but they share one primary concern, the desire to change the fate of the depression's victims. And they also share a pragmatic radicalism, a willingness to experiment with new methods and new techniques along with a belief that men create systems and that men are also capable of changing those systems. "Senator and Engineer" is a report on two speeches, the first by that old progressive, Senator Norris, whom Wilson obviously admires but who no longer possesses sufficient insight to understand exactly what is happening in depression America, a man bogged down in the rhetoric and battles of a progressivism long since out-of-date; the other, a speech given before the Taylor Society of Scientific Managers by H. J. Freyn, an engineer just returned from working on the construtcion of steel mills in the Soviet Union who is filled with admiration for Soviet methods as well as for the "unselfishness and integrity of . . . Soviet officials." It was men such as Freyn and Frank Keeney, the leader of an insurgent coal-miner's union, as well as William Z. Foster, to whom the future, if it was to be livable, must belong.

The American Jitters gains its structure from the geographical tragedy of the nation. The misery, the confusion, the despair and the hope to which the depression gave birth are sketched in these portraits of individual men and women. Between 1930 and the end of 1931, Wilson's confrontation with America pushed him further to the Left. The dehumanization that the depression brought to the surface of American life seemed inherent to capitalism. Traveling through the country, he had watched human lives atrophy beneath the weight of endemic poverty; he had felt the numbness and hopelessness that settled like fog across the American landscape; and he had seen the absurdity of hunger in the midst of plenty. The logic of life in America was its lack of logic, or at least its lack of a logic that could be considered civilized. His trip is similar to the one George Orwell was to make to Wigan Pier. What is most striking about the sketches in this book is Wilson's ability to communicate a sense of national catastrophe not through statistics but through stories of isolated human beings enmeshed in a terror that is as total as it seems incomprehensible. The artist's claim to humanity is challenged by the country through which he travels. The sympathy, the compassion, and the bitterness which Wilson brought to his travels in America remain today as the testimony of a great journalist.

Wilson's greatest facility as a writer is his ability to see history in distinctly personal terms. This is not the talent of the major novelist who manages to personalize discovery so that the reader feels that the novelist has inhabited that country inhabited by us all but recognized by the few. Wilson's talent is different. He absorbs history, but in making it personal he depersonalizes himself; one is somehow reminded of Trotsky. It is not with the author that he concludes *The American Jitters;* it is, rather, with "The Case of the Author." Wilson sees himself as representative of a class of cultivated, humane men. And when he writes, "So far as I can see, then, Karl Marx's predictions are in process of coming true," it is as an intellectual who has accepted Marxism as his future point of departure. Having been educated by his travels in depression America, he was to spend most of the following eight years examining Marx and the historical events Marx and other socialist thinkers helped to set in motion. Looking at America through the newly acquired Marxist lens, he employs Henry George and Charles Beard to testify to the accuracy of Marx's predictions about capitalism in America. In this very brief summation of Marxism and American history, one finds that same view of Marxism which was eventually to compose the sole consistent theme of *To the Finland Station.* For Wilson, Marxism develops from an economic base into an emotional desideratum. It is Marx's "psychological insight" that Wilson values, and it was to be the humanistic Marx—one is tempted to write the *artistic* Marx—whom Wilson was to find so appealing. "The truth is," he writes, "that economics is merely the study of how people behave about money, and Marx, although he possessed the true scholar's temperament and had all the statistics at his finger-tips, never lost sight of this fact. His great strength lay in his imaginative grasp of human history." From the first, Wilson concentrated on this aspect of Marx and Marxism. Here we have the first outlines of the "poet of commodities" whom we were to find "looking searchingly into . . . [his] heart" in *To the Finland Station.* In this brief note, Marx has already been divested of the "myth" of the dialectic and the labor theory of value to be ushered onto Wilson's stage in his role as another Hebrew light to the gentiles, one of the "great Jewish prophets."

But in *The American Jitters,* this is still subordinate to Wilson's view of the country: the cure to the depression is not to be found "in the charts of the compilers of statistics, but in one's self and in the people one sees." Wilson then turns to himself and to his family, offering his life "as a specimen of the current American bourgeoisie." In this, he is as much of a poseur as Henry Adams examining himself as a typical American in *The Education.* There is a certain quiet pride to his prose when he writes of how his mother's family "go back to the New England Mathers" and adds that his "father's and uncles' generation were obviously alienated by their old-fashioned education from the world of the great American money-making period." Like them, he has tried to accommodate himself to American capitalism without permitting himself to be "broken in to the world of machinery and enormous profits." But even in his attempts at resistance, he found himself "disciplined by that machinery and dazzled by those profits." He confesses to having disliked the era of America's dazzling prosperity, but he had, at the very same time, attempted to swallow the social and economic illusions it wished to perpetrate. Even prior to his discovery of the class issues involved, he had conceived a certain loathing for those elements in American life that saw, mirrored in their own superficiality, the culmination of western social and intellectual development. Now he finds himself "convinced that the money-making period of American history has definitely come to an end," and he frankly relishes the sight of "the well-to-do bankers, brokers, bond salesmen, stockholders and business men . . . no longer able to be fatuous on the same scale."

He hopes that the "emergency may produce its leaders," and envisions the rise to power of the technicians he has written about so sympathetically. That "such men are not democratic in the old American sense" and that "they do not believe in votes" does not seem particularly important. Like them, he admires "the Russian Communist leaders because they are men of superior brains who have triumphed over the ignorance, the stupidity and the shortsighted selfishness of the mass, who have imposed on them better methods and ideas than they could ever have arrived at by themselves." To sympathize with the new generation of radicals is not enough; Wilson urges his fellow intellectuals to ally themselves "with those elements who will remodel society by the power of imagination and thought." What he expects from the younger American radicals is a communism which will eliminate the insecurity embedded in capitalism, that will make such lives as those of the "dog-run" inhabitants of the Kentucky hills impossible.

Wilson's vision was far more evolutionary than it was utopian. He believed then—and apparently he still believes—in human development. Despite his distaste for industrial civilization, he never looked at the machine as enemy; the enemy was to remain those who controlled the machines for their own benefit. Henry Ford was his model of acquisitive man. And "The Case of the Author" is a strong argument with which to conclude a vivid series of close-ups of depression America. A coda consisting of a single paragraph entitled "The Man in the Street" follows, but it is simply intended as the final image of suffering and disintegration, a summation of the year Wilson had spent traveling through the country. Dos Passos probably had it in mind when he wrote the conclusion to *The Big Money.* The suffering and disintegration seem organized; life is at a standstill, a dead end; the country has run down; capitalism has played itself out; there is neither dream nor energy, and the man, a prisoner of some unknown past and the victim of the national myth of success, "wanders incongruously along West Fifty-eighth Street past the restaurants with smart French names and the half-empty apartment houses where liveried doormen guard the doors." *The American Jitters* encompasses the changes that the depression brought to the nation. After reading it, one understands why the greatest single effect of the depression was psychological rather than economic, why the American would never again be able to fuse his morality to his money. Fear was his newest legacy and the ebullient hope so characteristic of his life until 1929 had been destroyed. It is this shattering of the national myths that Wilson so magnificently records.

Granville Hicks once attributed Wilson's influence over other intellectuals to "his unequivocal desire for truth." The 1930s was the decade in which that desire was to be tested most severely. Wilson signed the manifesto called *Culture and the Crisis,* which called on intellectuals to support Foster and Ford, the Communist party's candidates for president and vice-president of the United States in 1932. Only "the overthrow of the system which is responsible for all crises" could create a culture characterized by human dignity and a lack of repression. There is, perhaps, no better barometer of how alienated American intellectuals had become by 1932 than to read this manifesto. What is most indicative of the degree of this alienation is that so many truly distinguished writers should have signed a document whose style was as cliché-ridden as its ideas were patent. It is difficult not to see in *Culture and the Crisis* a kind of mass catharsis designed to make intellectuals feel that they, too, were in the forefront of the resistance.

Wilson had praised Dreiser's *Tragic America* (a book which is decidedly inferior to *The American Jitters*) as an example of how a writer could undertake "the supremely important task of selling communism to the Americans," but he was already taking leave of the mentality of American communism. Truth remained truth and his alliance with American Communists was uncomfortable from the very beginning. He was never able to envelope himself in what he soon called "Marxist snow-blindness" and he quickly realized that it was impossible to "take Communism away from the Communists" because the party had so totally submerged its identity beneath that of its Soviet parent. Wilson was forced to define his relationship to his own vision rather than to permit that vision, comparable in the critic-journalist to the imaginative power of the poet or novelist, to become the property of any political group. He had recognized the problem in *Axel's Castle,* which concluded with an attempt to come to terms with it by advocating the creation of a different literature from the fusion of symbolist technique with objective reality. By 1933, Wilson was faced with an even more difficult problem, one that could not be looked at from an aesthetic point of view at all. Once he committed himself to an investigation of Marxism, he was forced to undertake the task of "hacking at the roots of his own belief." Hyman's condemnation of Wilson for doing this makes little sense, since the ability to question one's own beliefs remains an intellectual obligation for the critic or historian. To Wilson's credit, he forced himself to look at Marxism as the ideal critic would look at drama. Marxism, too, contained its human struggle, and by 1933 Wilson had begun to look at that struggle as it was being enacted by Trotsky and Stalin. His sympathies were with the exiled Jewish intellectual.

It is strange that we still possess no adequate study of Trotsky's influence upon modern intellectuals. Wilson was one of the first American intellectuals to identify himself with the most Promethean of twentieth-century Marxism's dethroned gods. One suspects that it is this identification which made him take Max Eastman seriously long after most intellectuals had simply dismissed Eastman. More than any other figure except Lenin, Trotsky seemed to him the individual whose life had been constructed around the Marxist idea. The combination of man of action and man of letters had already proved intriguing when he dealt with Rimbaud in *Axel's Castle.* It was to prove just as intriguing when he discovered Malraux or wrote about Trotsky. To create one's individual identity around a "philosophical system which leads directly to action" had immense appeal for an intellectual who lived in a world that had little use for the intellectual.

The writers who now began to interest him share with Marx, Engels, Lenin and Trotsky a fundamental alienation from bourgeoise culture. Even Dickens, James, and Flaubert, who represent nonrevolutionary western culture in *The Triple Thinkers* and *The Wound and the Bow*, have a great deal in common with the portrait of Marx that emerges from *To The Finland Station.* In Trotsky, he found a man of action and of thought who had consciously turned himself into "an instrument of history," but even by 1933 it was already apparent that Trotsky's remarkable talents would not be equal to the narrower but more functional talents of men whose capacities were primarily organizational. Throughout the thirties, Wilson's work was, in large part, a debate he conducted between the humanism and authoritarianism which soon seemed endemic to Marx himself. Stalin eventually became for him, as he did for so many other ex-Marxists, the deus-ex-machina killer of the Marxist dream. Wilson's growing skepticism about where orthodox Marxism seemed to be headed was voiced in *Travels in Two Democracies* and *The Triple Thinkers,* the two books which preceeded *To the Finland Station.*

The fact that *Travels in Two Democracies* is not as successful a book as *The American Jitters* can only be attributed to Wilson's growing political confusion. The impressionistic technique which had served him so well in 1931 seems strained and unsuited to what he is trying to create. It deprives him of a focus, where it had earlier forced the reader to inhabit the world he was writing about. Even more damaging to the book's total effect is that Wilson was unable to incorporate his American and Russian travels so that they highlighted each other. The book seems to be two separate works that have simply been printed together, and when he came to republish them in the 1950s Wilson worked them into two different collections of his journalism: the first half of *Travels* was printed along with the material from *The*

American Jitters and some previously uncollected pieces in a book called *The American Earthquake;* the second half, covering his travels in the Soviet Union from May to October 1935 was reprinted in *Red, Black, Blond and Olive.* It included some material, most of it anti-Soviet, which Wilson had deliberately left out of *Travels in Two Democracies.*

Wilson was unable to reconcile what he wanted as a Marxist with American life in the early days of the New Deal. The American chapters of *Travels* cover the period from November 1932 to May 1934. His description of the "Inaugural Parade" is characteristic of the book's lack of focus. Roosevelt is blurred against the background of Washington's stagnancy. The parade itself is an anachronism for America is no longer the country of "the great barbecue." Bad omens abound; people are "dreary" and "curiously apathetic." And the inaugural address, which today certainly seems one of the better inaugural addresses made by an American president, he dismisses as being filled with "shadowy" phrases and the "old pulpit vagueness" and "unctuousness." "There is a warning, itself rather vague, of a possible dictatorship."

Wilson's tendency to dramatize history through individuals was less than fortunate when he came to write about Roosevelt, an individual toward whom he possesses a curiously violent antipathy. As the New Deal progressed and as orthodox Marxism came to seem less attractive, he began, at first quite grudgingly, to recognize that Roosevelt had succeeded in restoring a sense of vitality to American life. But even in a "Postscript of 1957," which he attached to *The American Earthquake,* Roosevelt is a flaccid weak-willed potential demagogue with "certain tendencies in common" with Hitler and Stalin. If Lenin is the stuff of drama for him, then Roosevelt is the stuff of caricature, a Machiavellian comic-strip character insidiously plotting to force the country into war.

With the exception of "Hull House in 1932," with its deeply moving description of Jane Addams, and of the remarkable essay entitled "The Old Stone House," the American section of Wilson's *Travels* leaves a great deal to be desired. One does not sense that its author was in contact with what was happening in the country as he was in 1931. Perhaps his immersion in the intellectual origins and growth of socialism made it even more difficult for him to close in on what he was seeing between 1932 and 1934. With the exception of "The Old Stone House," there is a perceptible impatience that the writer feels for his subject matter. In "The Old Stone House," Wilson once again explores the history of his family, this time by creating a geography of motion in which the family house in Talcottville assumes the dimensions of the America still to be explored. But this was not the exploration he was intent upon in his *Travels.*

Wilson's Russian pilgrimage is somewhat more interesting, but it is equally static, probably because by 1935 his doubts about the direction of the Soviet experiment were already quite serious. He is not really able to comit himself to the Soviet Union, just as he was unable to commit himself to New Deal America. If Roosevelt had become the barrier preventing him from endorsing the New Deal, then the figure of Stalin began to loom larger and larger in his writing about the Soviet Union. His distrust of Stalin is balanced, in part, by a desire to believe that Russian society works. He liked the Russians he met, but he liked them because they were "natural and frank, like Americans." Both are unlike the English, and it is almost with relief that Wilson gives vent to his anglophobia, as he dismisses England as "stale" and "fading," an old country in which "Shakespeare seemed a long time ago."

Only in Leningrad is he truly comfortable. For Leningrad possesses an artistic spirit which seeks to combine whatever can be salvaged from the prerevolutionary past with the idealism of the revolution's patron saint. Lenin himself is eulogized as Wilson describes the statue of the Soviet St. Paul which stands in front of the opera house.

But in Moscow, Wilson is reduced to celebrating the glories of the newly opened Moscow subway which, he discovers, is "the only *pretty* subway in the world." In what is presumably a line intended as sarcasm, he writes, "When the subway was opened, Comrade Stalin, who can take it, rode the escalator twice in succession." Straining to confirm belief, he finds in Moscow a society which possesses "a more rational base and a nobler aim" than American society. But he does not deny the tensions and problems which are visible in the Soviet state, although he does seek to excuse them by insisting that they are no more than the unavoidable consequences bound to disturb any social experiment. The presence of the secret police cannot be avoided, but, seeking to avoid the logic of his own observations, he asks whether they are any worse than the police in American industrial towns. But the contradictions between the ideal and the reality remain: the people to whom he spoke "always looked over their shoulders before venturing to say anything about politics." His "Final Reflections" about the Soviet Union are hesitant and unsure, as if he were still trying to absorb the contradictions he witnessed. He salutes the "extraordinary heroism" of Soviet life, but for the first time since the depression he does not call for the American equivalent of the Soviet dictatorship. He now feels convinced that "American republican institutions . . . have some permanent and absolute value."

And there is still Lenin. Lenin in his "tomb under the Kremlin wall" symbolizes the spirit which, Wilson insists, still infuses the builders of Soviet society. It is Lenin's presence, even in death, which makes Russia "the moral top of the world." And it is Lenin who had seen "all those triumphs to which life must rise and to which he thought himself but a guidepost." But even so eloquent a tribute to the greatness of Lenin is not enough to provide *Travels in Two Democracies* with any coherent social philosophy. The book, intended to depict two conflicting but dynamic cultures, depicts instead its author's moral confusion. And the trap into which Wilson falls is at least partially of his own making.

If *The Triple Thinkers*, published two years later, is a better book that is because its mood is so much more decisively honest. F. O. Matthiessen, in a review, called it the product of a "disturbed and disillusioned radical," but such a statement probably tells us more about Matthiessen's own intellectual struggles at the time than it does about *The Triple Thinkers*. For here his investigations into Marxism as well as his travels in the United States and Russia have been absorbed into his criticism. Wilson consciously took his title from Flaubert for the express purpose of acknowledging the artist's moral necessities, which precede his allegiance to any political system.

With the exception of some of the material included in the essay on Henry James and "The Satire of Samuel Butler," all of the essays collected in *The Triple Thinkers* were written after Wilson's return from the Soviet Union and his break with Stalinism. And the collected essays represent a curious reversion back to the absolute atristic independence which he had, at least by implication, attacked in *Axel's Castle*. What is curious is that Wilson takes to this position the tools which his intensive study of Marxism offered. On the one hand the responsibility of the artist is served by his truthful expression of his own view of reality; on the other, the artist is a creature of his class. His artistic vision is itself a class product. In all of these essays, the conception of class as the decisive factor in literary creation can be seen.

The book itself, put together while Wilson was in the throes of a furious anti-Stalinism, attempts to examine literature from the vantage point of Marxist theory. But Wilson possessed the happy facility of de-emphasizing the very idea which had provided his critical impetus. To transform what he takes into what he needs is among those criteria by means of which we measure a critic's persuasive power. In *The Triple Thinkers*, Wilson uses what he has learned about class as a psychologically centrifugal force in the life of any artist, but he also uses his very wide range of reading and scholarship. One sees the combination not only in those essays which are directly political, such as "The Politics of Flaubert" or "Bernard Shaw at Eighty," but in the essay on Housman. Wilson sets Housman in "the monastic order of English university ascetics," along with Walter Pater, Lewis Carroll, and Edward Fitzgerald, but he then concludes by measuring the rigidity of Housman's work, even his best work, with the breadth and power of Heine's. No one would consider this a major critical feat, just as no one would consider the essay one of Wilson's superior critical performances; but, after reading it, no one can dismiss Housman as a dull and uninteresting minor poet. Wilson once described his intentions as a critic as "either to present some writer who was not well enough known or, in the case of a familiar writer, to call attention to some neglected aspect of his work or his career." Having had nothing very "fresh" to say about "the pathos of *The Shropshire Lad*," he focuses his attention on "the classical scholarship of Housman in its bearing on his poetry and personality." And he remains one of the few critics writing in English capable of performing such a task.

Even in the two poorest essays in this collection, "The Ambiguity of Henry James" and "Is Verse a Dying Technique?" he is able to offer us new points of comparison which show us a writer or a literary tendency as we have never seen them before. The approach is invaluable. For while criticism may be the stepchild of philosophy, one should acknowledge that it is only the stepchild. When Wilson forces *The Turn of the Screw* into a Freudian mold, he is guilty of imposing his thesis on his readers. But once he gets away from that to speak of the work of James's later years and particularly of James's relationship to America (especially when he calls attention to James's "magnificient phrase about Lincoln's 'mold-smashing mask' " and we are reminded of the growing importance the Civil War and Lincoln himself were to have on Wilson's own work) and to his social class, he succeeds in creating a new view of James for the reader. Wilson admires James; he does not worship him. When he writes of James's limitations as a novelist, we are aware of how firm his critical grip is. James is singular in American fiction, but his singularity is, in part, the product of the limitations of his sympathies. Even today, parts of Wilson's essay offer the reader a well-rounded assessment of James, especially for those readers who, like Wilson, believe that *The Bostonians* rather than *The Ambassadors* represents James at his most fulfilled if not his most individual pitch.

In the light of Wilson's own evolution, one can see in *The Triple Thinkers* an intellectual parody of the Marxist dialectic, which Wilson had already dismissed as a religious myth in 1937. Admittedly, it is a parody given vitality by that which it seeks to ridicule. The essays on Housman, James, and Flaubert explore writers whose chief concern was with putting to work their individual vision and whose work had little reformist motivation. The essays on Paul Elmer More, on "Marxism and Literature," and on George Bernard Shaw present an antithesis in which the artist's vision is subservient to a moral or political ideal. And in Wilson's former Hill School teacher, Mr. Rolfe (the teacher as artist), and in John Jay Chapman, we are given the synthesis: the fusion of artistic integrity and social consciousness which together create the moral-artistic point of view. The artist is, indeed, a moralist, but he can surrender his art to no single dogma.

One can, of course, argue that Wilson had been doing this from his very beginnings as a literary critic and that it is, as a matter of fact, this very trait which he shares with the New Humanists that has been seized upon by those of his critics who charge him with ignoring a work of art's form. But his immersion in Marxism gave Wilson, among other things, a more settled view of the relationship of literature and history: the vision of the artist came to seem more and more singular. The figures with whom he is most sympathetic in *The Triple Thinkers* share the positive independence of the artist.

That Wilson was able to take a great deal away from his study of Marxism is evident in the best essays in *The Triple Thinkers.* The political idealism of the early thirties was chipped away by the political realities he observed in the United States and the Soviet Union. But his criticism emerges as something tougher. In "The Politics of Flaubert," for instance, one is struck by the forceful manner with which Wilson develops his conception of Flaubert as a potential social critic who was—until forced by the shock of the Paris Commune to fall back on the petit bourgeois prejudices and habits of mind of his class—moving toward the same revelations as Marx. Flaubert's answers to the problems plaguing French society seem decidedly similar to the answers of Marx. But Wilson is not interested in providing us with a Marxist analysis of Flaubert. What he wants to do is reverse this and analyze Marxism through Flaubert's, the artist's, eyes. If Marx possessed the prescription which might free the artist and the worker alike, then Flaubert anticipated certain dangers which seem inherent in Marxism. Wilson's description of the role Sénécal plays in *L'Éducation Sentimentale* is written both with Flaubert's novel and his own journey through the Soviet Union in mind. For Sénécal is the prototype of authoritarian man, as much a part of our century as the automobile, and we recognize in him that individual whose "behavior as a policeman and . . . yearnings toward socialist control are both derived from his impulse toward despotism." Wilson had already adopted the position that he was to voice more fully in *To the Finland Station,* that the authoritarianism of Marxism derives from Marx himself. Sénécal becomes the figure in whom the socialist ideal turns in upon itself. And if there is any affirmation of the supremacy of art over politics in Wilson's work, it is in this essay. Flaubert has been able to perceive what has eluded historical science. The artist breaks the grip of dogma through his ability to embrace nothing but that which lives; the true triple thinker owes allegiance to "neither religion nor fatherland nor even any social conviction."

This is not to suggest that Wilson sees Flaubert, or any artist, for that matter, as an alternative to Marx: it is simply that he now recognizes the artist as the man who stands outside. It is only when Flaubert reacts so violently to the commune uprisings that he himself leaves the ranks of the triple thinkers, for he then turns in fear and horror against even the idea of the revolution of the proletariat. Flaubert is an artist, but he is also a political consciousness limited by his class and background. If there is any alternative to Marx in *The Triple Thinkers*, then it is the American, John Jay Chapman.

Two other essays, "Marxism and Literature" and "Bernard Shaw at Eighty," reflect Wilson's growing disillusionment with the development of contemporary Marxism and with the authoritarian temperament in general. In the first of these, he challenges the entire body of Marxist literary patois by examining what Marx, Engels, Lenin, and Trotsky had actually written about literature. He is ready to admit that art can be made "an effective instrument in the class struggle," but this does not change the essential fact that the effectiveness of a work of art depends not upon its propagandistic but upon its aesthetic values. The essay is more persuasive in its rhetoric than in its logic. It is historically inaccurate. Wilson is locked into his own contradictions, for he sees in a writer such as Malraux a distinct product of the Marxist "vision of history" (a doubtful proposition today) and ultimately is forced into defining Marxism itself as "the first efforts of the human spirit to transcend literature itself." If it were accurate, the statement would destroy the necessity for literary criticism as well as the necessity of art itself; as rhetoric, it is merely embarrassing.

And yet "Marxism and Literature" remains stimulating and refreshing for anyone who has worked his way through the tendentious literary philosophizing with which American Marxism in particular seems to have been plagued. Wilson can attack such pedantry from the dual vantage point of a sympathy, however limited, for Marxism and a knowledge of what literature is about and what it does. In the same way, the essay on Shaw enables the reader to see Shaw in an entirely new relation to society. Shaw, too, is among the policemen of socialism: like Sénécal, he is intrigued by power and he identifies not with a political ideal but with any "superior person" capable of bringing "the Idea" into being. Shaw is a peculiar mixture of pamphleteer and artist. And just as a journalist such as Lincoln Steffens is capable of lumping together Ford, Mussolini, and Lenin as images of the new man, without ever grasping the substantial differences in their aims, so Shaw can praise Mussolini, Hitler, and Stalin as men who are capable of getting things done, at the very same time that he dismisses Hitler's anti-Semitism as "a bee in his bonnet" and accepts Stalin's liquidation of the old Bolsheviks "on the principle that the socially harmful had to be got out of the way."

The single most important essay in *The Triple Thinkers*, at least for what it pointed toward in Wilson's own development, is that on John Jay Chapman. Like "The Old Stone House," it reflects Wilson's growing struggle to derive strength from the Protestant world of his ancestors. As he resurrects a virtually forgotten man of letters, the values from which he himself was to derive sustenance once Marxism had failed him as a philosophy begin to seem evident. From this time on, much of his best work was to concern itself with members of his family, with the American past, and with a style of life and intellect which today seems as attractive as it is vestigial.

The essay is also an example of Wilson's ability to rescue an attractive figure from obscurity. It is an attempt, in large part succesful, to create renewed interest in a writer Wilson felt had been unfairly neglected. He is not, here, introducing a new writer to the American reading public, as he did in his early reviews of Hemingway, Malraux, and Henry Miller. He is, rather, trying to bring before the reading public a writer so old-fashioned as to be new. Wilson possesses great confidence in the vitality of the moral imagination, and while he discriminates between the achievements of Tolstoy and Cable, of Dante and Chapman, he approaches them with a strong sense of each writer's singularity. It is from Chapman and Mr. Rolfe, as it is later to be from his father, that Wilson takes a renewed belief in the individual's debt to himself. Each of them brings to life a standard of integrity. After years of trying to make Marx's vision his own, Wilson returns to a more personalized idea of what life is all about. Chapman's refusal to compromise intrigues him. And he finds in the spectacle of John Jay Chapman protesting the burning alive of a Negro in a small Pennsylvania town a historical moment that is, in its own way, as meaningful as Lenin's speech at the Finland Station.

But it is Marx to whom, like a monk shriving himself of the errors of the flesh, Wilson is obliged to return—Marx and the world Marx helped bring into being. *To the Finland Station*, which was published in 1940, seven years after Wilson began work on it, is neither a historical study nor a critique of the development of Marxism, although Wilson claims to do both these things. It is, instead, a work of art cast in the form of a study of history and it owes as much to Wilson's dramatic imagination as it does to his historical investigations. It is Wilson's finest book, one of the very few books written about socialism as an evolving historical force which enable the reader to see it within its strictly human dimensions. Marxism loses a great deal of its historical inevitability when Wilson scrutinizes it, but it gains a different ascendency. *To the Finland Station* would make far more sense to today's New Leftists than it did to many of Wilson's contemporaries when it was published. At the book's conception, Wilson was himself a

Marxist, a man who envisoned an American communism; by the time he finished it, he had become not only disillusioned with Marxism as a political system but more aware of Marxism as a political currency, distinctly contemporary, overwhelmingly of this world.

In the seven years that it took him to write *To the Finland Station,* Wilson underwent a personal political metamorphosis. That his philosophy of Marxism is inconsistent with his politics in the early 1930s is obvious, but this was, far from being a hinderance, perhaps his greatest asset in the writing of the book. The philosophy shifted, but the dramatic point of view remained. By the time the book was finished, Wilson called himself a democratic socialist. He announced his intention to vote for Norman Thomas in 1940 in a line that might describe his own labors on *To the Finland Station:* "he is the old-fashioned kind of Socialist, but he has come through this period of confusion on the Left with a record that shines in the dark night." If his enthusiasm for communism withered away during the seven years that he worked on *To the Finland Station,* his sense of the need to break through the causes of human oppression remained.

Behind "the spotlighting method" with which Wilson depicts the development of socialism stands the figure who is not among the historical actors whom Wilson sketches in these pages. The dark, melodramatic presence of Stalin manipulates the destruction of Marxist morality, although the seeds of that destruction have already been planted by Marx himself. Wilson held his distrust of Stalin in check until 1937, by which time he was openly attacking the Soviet leader for having constructed from history an ideological catechism that made the defense of "so many falsehoods" an intellectual act of faith for the true believer. By 1937, Wilson was convinced that Russia under Stalin was moving "in the direction of fascism," and he accurately predicted in 1937 that Stalin would soon be Hitler's ally. Just as he had come to identify the "moral vision" of Marxism with

Lenin and Trotsky, so he came to identify Russian authoritarianism with Stalin. But Wilson was Manichaean in his desire to substitute, or at least to blame, the historical devil for the historical god.

The totalitarian strains which seen endemic to Marxism presented Wilson with a number of problems. He was unable to dismiss them, and yet he still wished to salvage as much from Marxist morality as he possibly could. He was confused about the relationship of Marxism to the Soviet state. On the one hand, he believed that Russia had surrendered its role as caretaker of the Marxist vision of history and that the decline of Marxism in the Soviet Union would produce the beneficial effect of relieving Marxists of "the moral authority of Russia." On the other hand, he was, like so many of his fellow intellectuals, in the intellectual trap of having so firmly identified Marxism with what was happening in Russia that its moral superiority came to possess less and less meaning for him as his recognition of Soviet tyranny grew. He reminds one of Trotsky, who, although he came close to so doing in his unfinished life of Stalin, was never able to ascribe Russian authoritarianism to the Party apparatus originally set up by Lenin but was, instead, satisfied to excoriate Stalin as a demagogic pretender who had no real claim to leadership over the Communist world. Like so many other ex-Marxists Wilson wished to believe that Marxism had nothing to do with the political system of the Soviet Union. But like these men, too, he was caught up in the contradictions which seem inherent in Marx's own thought. Rosa Luxemborg was among the earliest to note that the dictatorship of the proletariat would probably mean a dictatorship over the proletariat. In the Soviet Union, such a dictatorship had been instituted by Lenin, adhered to by Trotsky, and taken over by Stalin. Stalin was the logical meeting ground of the ideas of Marx and the actions of Lenin. Wilson hints at this in *To the Finland Station*, but he still admires Lenin far too much to surrender the myth of Manichaean Stalinism. Interestingly enough, Isaac Deutscher, in his three-volume biography of Trotsky, saw Stalin's role in the revolution with greater clarity than either Wilson or Trotsky. Lenin's emphasis on the necessity of strong party leadership negated whatever use the Bolsheviks themselves had had for the creativity of the masses. The fact that Lenin possessed so many attractive personal qualities and that he was among the greatest men of our century should not have prevented Wilson from seeing this.

In *To the Finland Station,* Wilson tries to develop the theme of how authoritarianism is inherent to Marxism, but he was working under the distinct handicap of having given tacit endorsement to just such authoritarianism himself. Had he not, in the first flushes of his own Marxist enthusiasm, disavowed being "democratic in the old American sense"? And had he not praised Stalin and the other Russian leaders for having "triumphed over the shortsighted selfishness of the mass" by imposing "on them better methods and ideas than they could ever have arrived at themselves"? What he was vehemently objecting to by 1937 was virtually identical with what he had praised, almost as vehemently, in 1932—the prerogatives of absolute power.

The chief reason why *To the Finland Station* is an imaginative rather than a historical study is that Wilson responds to the appeal of personality far more than he responds to the appeal of ideas. Even his metaphors show the extent to which he thinks of power in terms of personality alone: Trotsky is "the young eagle"; Lenin "the great headmaster"; Marx himself moves from the combination of "Prometheus and Lucifer" to "the poet of commodities."

To the Finland Station is among the most moving accounts of the origins of contemporary socialism that we have. Wilson wrote it at the height of his powers as a writer and he integrates the personalities of socialism's thinkers and actors with their backgrounds. In examining a development in Western thought which has already changed the face of the world and which may yet change our idea of what constitutes a civilization, as well as in enabling us to see the men who are largely responsible for this, *To the Finland Station* has not really been surpassed. The artist possesses what the political analyst describes and deciphers. Wilson's two chapters on Trotsky leave the reader with a better sense of the style and personality of the dethroned claimant than do all three volumes of Deutscher's remarkably thorough biography. Controlled and sure of himself as a writer, Wilson instinctively meets the dramatic moment with the correct phrase. In no other book was he so absolutely in command of his prose, not even in *The American Jitters* or *Patriotic Gore*. Nowhere else, not even in *Axel's Castle*, was he better at matching the power of historical ideas and historical figures with his own power as a writer. His metaphors grow out of his characters. Marx is "the poet of commodities" because Wilson reads him as a great imaginative artist struggling with his materials:

> These writings of Marx are electrical. Nowhere perhaps in the history of thought is the reader so made to feel the excitement of a new intellectual discovery. Marx is here at his most vivid and his most vigorous—in the closeness and exactitude of political observation; in the energy of the faculty that combines, articulating at the same time that it compresses; in the wit and the metaphorical phantasmagoria that transfigures the prosaic phenomena of politics, and in the pulse of the tragic invective—we have heard its echo in Bernard Shaw—which can turn the collapse of an incompetent parliament, divided between contradictory tendencies, into the downfall of a damned soul of Shakespeare.

The chapter which extends "the great headmaster" metaphor to characterize all of Lenin's life is a model of the poetic clarity available only to the finest historical writers. Wilson conceives of history as an "art-science," but he writes it solely as an artist. One senses that it is the artist which appeals to him in Michelet, in Marx himself, in the exiled Trotsky. And just as in *The American Jitters* he is able to write so movingly of the dispossessed and hungry, here it is the figure of the exile which attracts him, especially the exiled intellectual. One suspects that he had already begun to think of himself as living in a kind of exile.

To the Finland Station opens with an examination of the bourgeois revoultionary tradition as it was created in the work of the great French historian, Michelet, and as it declined in the work of Renan, Taine, and Anatole France. Michelet's passion for human freedom is the best that the bourgeoisie have to offer, but once their class, for whom Michelet is chosen as the intellectual spokesman, has attained its own freedom it destroys its revolutionary heritage by becoming the oppressor of the working class. As Wilson traces it for us in a series of restrained but dramatic episodes, Michelet's passion disintegrates and the revolutionary tradition comes full circle to the sight of its own fearfulness, its flaccid yet frenetic resistance to the rise of a new class which forces it to oppose the revolutionary thrust of the socialist world.

But this is merely the frame for the picture of the socialist revolutionary tradition. For it is socialism which has come to disturb the modern world and socialism which had irrevocably stamped its presence on the modern intellectual. Once again utilizing his instinct for the dramatic as he was unable to do in his plays, Wilson casts socialism's origins into a courtroom, where the French revolutionary, Gracchus Babeuf, is on trial for his life. An impassioned Babeuf defends the proposed insurrection of his Society of Equals against an exhausted government which itself was soon to relinquish the French future into the hands of Napoleon; his movement will lead to social and economic equality and will destroy all barriers to a Christian society. Babeuf's socialism becomes for us an extension of Christian ethics into political activity, but it is his speech to the court which

Wilson singles out as the birth of the socialist tradition in Europe. For the speech highlights that moment in history when the French Revolution had become the property of a new owning class and Babeuf himself looks both backward and forward. "His defense," writes Wilson, "is like a summing-up of the unrealized ideals of the Enlightenment and a vindication of their ultimate necessity."

The rise of socialism is, naturally, most concerned with the work of Marx and Engels. But from Babeuf, in an effort to show us how the socialist tradition took root, Wilson guides us briefly through the thought and lives of Saint-Simon, Proudhon, Fourier, Owen, Enfantin, and the American utopians. But where Wilson was successful in depicting Babeuf's uniqueness (he seems to combine the best qualities of Lenin and Shelley), here he becomes, to a large extent, the victim of his method and his imaginative grasp of history. Enfantin, for example, was undoubtedly "bizarre," but was he really in the mainstream of the revolutionary tradition? Is he really among the thinkers who create socialism? Or is he not a man enmeshed in his own colorful career, content to exist on the peripheries of socialism as he would have been content to exist on the peripheries of any movement which came to the forefront in his time? And the psychological probing of both Enfantin and Saint-Simon remind one that Wilson is in midstride as a writer, that he has not wholly reconciled the influence of Freud with the influence of Marx for purposes of his own art.

In these early chapters, his purpose seems to be to trace the development of a new religion, founded, like Christianity, on the age-old desire for equality among men. The conflict between the socialist ideal—from its origins at war with the Calvinist ideal which nestled into the capitalist ethos—and the instinctive acquisitiveness of capitalism springs from ideas circulated by socialism's early thinkers and actors. Many of those ideas were incorporated into the elaborate system which Marx and Engels created; from their introduction into Marxism, they were to feed socialism's historical actors, Bakunin, Lassalle, Lenin, and Trotsky.

In his description of the milieu from which Marx arose to create the system that bears his name, Wilson is far better than in the sketches of the early socialist thinkers. He subjects Marx's life to a far clearer analysis than he was to subject the lives of the writers with whom he dealt in *The Wound and the Bow*, his most overtly Freudian book. Wilson seizes on the essential metaphorical construction—what Kenneth Burke would call the "strategy" of his book—in his picture of Prometheus, the bearer of light, at war with Lucifer, the most single-minded of all rebels; together, they are fused in a nineteenth-Century biblical ramrod. The metaphor comes to dominate not merely Marx but the socialist idea itself. For Wilson, Marx is the product of a secularized Hebraism. However debatable this may be as history, it liberates Marx from so much of what has been written about him. Wilson has created the artist's Marx, a Marx who exists as a man and as a thinker. And the reader watches in fascination as he applies the same intellectual discipline his ancestors applied to their rabbinical studies to the study of the relationships of men to society.

Wilson ascribes too much to Marx's Jewishness. Occasionally, he is guilty of such dubious assertions as "nobody but a Jew could have fought so uncompromisingly and obstinately for the victory of the dispossessed classes." And yet the portrait of Marx that emerges is more than powerful; it roots out what is most essential to Marx and permits us to see it. The reader wants to believe in Wilson's Marx, so compelling is this Old Testament patriarch embodying the moral genius of his age in his own person and forcing his own sense of righteousness on the stiff-necked bourgeoisie of Europe. It is only after one rereads *To the Finland Station* that one becomes uncomfortable with the portrait's accents. Was it his rabbinical heritage which made Marx so financially irresponsible about his family? Was it the rabbinical heritage which enabled him to avoid facing the question of why socialism would bring with it the millennial future? Was it his "Old Testament sterness" which blinded him to the human qualities of friends and compatriots until even Engels was on the verge of breaking with him? Was it in keeping with his role as patriarch to break his followers on the rack of his own personal insecurity? And why should the emancipated nineteenth-century Jew possess a particularly Hebraic moral outlook, especially when, as in Marx's case, he is apparently more the product of the ideas of Ricardo, Hegel, and the pre-Marxist socialists than he is of secularized Judaism? It is an excellent portrait, but one suspects that the thesis is too dramatically compelling to be wholly accurate.

The drama is heightened as Wilson turns his attention to the historical actors as they move into the socialist camp. Bakunin, Lassalle, Lenin, Trotsky—all are driven toward socialism, and what drives them, we are made to feel, is a deep inscrutable hatred of the older order. One cannot read *To the Finland Station* without experiencing an almost religious awe as Wilson depicts what such men were capable of doing to their own lives. When Wilson draws Lenin, a gentle man by nature, living with an inflexible determination to break the old order and to make of himself a tool of revolution whose function is to impose his will—and not even his will but what he thinks of as Marx's—on those surrounding him until they, too, are mere instruments of history, the reader feels the Marxist ideal as a power ruling life through its own excruciating intensity. To Lenin, there comes "the word of Marx to add to his moral conviction the certainty that he was carrying out one of the essential tasks of human history." The patriarch chooses his descendent, as Moses chooses Joshua, and he chooses him through the power of the word. As Wilson describes it, we see that Lenin's superiority to the society in which he matures is more than a personal superiority; to recognize one's historical role is either to be transformed or to be mad. His fate is thrust on him, almost like sainthood.

> Vladimir, released, becomes Lenin. The Son of the Councillor of State divests himself of his social identity, assumes the anti-social character of a conspiritor; and in graduating into the world-view of Marxism, he even partly loses his identity as a Russian and is occupied with lines of force that make of national boundaries conventions and extend through the whole human world.

It is a book filled with brilliant portraits. And it brings to Marxism the vital independence of the artist, which, in turn, leads both to stimulating insights and dubious assertions. When he rejected dialectical materialism and the labor theory of value, he stripped his consciousness of the morality which had originally impelled him in his journey into Marxism. It was a courageous gesture for which he was, strangely enough, condemned—and it remains in our time an example of an intellectual accepting responsibility for his thoughts as well as for his actions. *To the Finland Station* brought to its conclusion in the days of the Hitler-Stalin pact, is a disavowal of Marxism as a philosophy which continues to insist that Marx's thought be used as a source of observation, analysis, and moral probing. In certain respects, it will appear more contemporary to the reader today than it did when it was published in 1940, for the Marx about whom Wilson writes most sympathetically is the young Marx who probed the causes of man's alienation and found them in the rigid inhumanity of nineteenth-century capitalism.

Wilson rejected the idea that Marxism had to be defended as a closed philosophical system when he rejected the dialectic an an inviolable historical law. Defense of the dialectic and the labor theory of value seemed intellectually constricting, something like the defense of the philosophy of Thomas Acquinas carried out in a computer center. Of the dialectic, he would go no further than to admit that Marx had made "effective use of it to exhibit the impossibilities of capitalism and to demonstrate the necessity for socialism." Ultimately, however, it was just one more "religious myth, disencumbered of divine personality and tied up with the history of mankind." Whether or not Wilson's assessment of the dialectic and the labor theory of value is valid is not as important for our purposes as the fact that he departed from orthodox Marxism in much the same manner as he came to it: systems remained as tenable as the morality of the men behind them. Perhaps the best summation of Wilson's 1940 position was offered fifteen years later in Milovan Djilas's *The New Class.*

> The world has seen few heroes as ready to sacrifice and suffer as the Communists were on the eve of and during the revolution. It has probably never seen such characterless wretches and stupid defenders of arid formulas as they became after attaining power. Wonderful human features were the condition for creating and attracting power for the movement; exclusive caste spirit and complete lack of ethical principles and virtues have become conditions for the power and maintenance of the movement.

In departing from Marxism, Wilson remained highly sympathetic toward the insights of that Marx whose economic observations created the poetry of commodities. This was the Marx upon whom Wilson focused. In *To the Finland Station,* he describes the theoretical weaknesses of *Das Kapital,* then points out that its greatness as a book is the greatness of any important work of art: it extends man's moral imagination. Perhaps this is one of Wilson's weaknesses as a social critic. No longer able to look at Marxism as a cure for society's ills, he now conceived of it as morality alone. Dismissing the dialectic and the labor theory of value, he culled from Marx's system the Hebraic vision of its founder as that vision had been modified by Lenin's "idealism."

The stress on Marxist "idealism" has the effect of, in part, making a Babeuf out of Marx. One senses that Wilson had to fight the impulse to make of Marxism a poetic metaphor which is simply an echo of the age-old desire to establish a just and humane society on this earth. Certainly, in choosing the poet in Marx over the economic theorist, Wilson can be accused of stripping Marxism of its vitality in order to applaud its humanitarian instincts. The "moral integrity" with which he endows Marxism is somehow too vast for him to track down; he was on surer, if narrower, ground when he turned to the moral integrity of John Jay Chapman.

Just as Wilson stresses that Marxism as it was conceived has little to do with what is happening in Stalinist Russia, so he develops, at the book's end, a new conception of the United States, a country whose development he views as alien to Marx's understanding. For what Marx was unable to see was "that the absence in the United States of the feudal class background of Europe would have the effect not only of facilitating the expansion of capitalism but also of making possible a genuine social democratization." American class structure remains fluid, since it is "mainly based on money, and the money is always changing hands so rapidly that the class lines cannot get cut very deeply." And not only does the United States possess a standard of living that the socialist world is still seeking, it has also acquired what "other peoples will learn to want and will get: free movement and a fair amount of free speech." It is the United States rather than the Soviet Union which now stands at "the moral top of the world." That same America which he had believed was dying in 1931 was now the moral standard for political states. It had been a long journey and if he was to find himself celebrated for coming home, he was also to find that the absence of what Marxism had provided him with was to turn him into a writer far too intent on the geography of personality. The essays in *The Triple Thinkers* owe their power to the fact that Wilson was wrestling with his own private and public personalities in the name of Marxism. That the essays in *The Wound and the Bow* are generally weaker seems obvious. It is not that Wilson deserted Marx for Freud. It is simply that he, like so many intellectuals, functioned better with faith—even with the doubt faith provides—than he did without it.

The thirties was Wilson's most creative decade. Beginning with *Axel's Castle* in 1931 and ending with *To the Finland Station* in 1940, he brought to his writing as a critic, as a journalist, and as a historian not merely remarkable insight and scholarship but a deep passion which he was never again to match. His inability to replace the vision of the "truly human" culture which he found in Marxism did not result in disillusionment but in disconnection, a movement away from the common life and a retreat into the increasingly private lanes of his own consciousness. Nothing that Wilson wrote after *To the Finland Station* provided him with the language for his passion that he needed, not even *Patriotic Gore.* And not even in the chapters on Lincoln and Grant or Holmes in *Patriotic Gore* or in "The Author at Sixty" in *A Piece of my Mind* was he to match his portrait of Marx.

And never again was he to bring to his writing the kind of social impetus that a worldwide protest movement inspired in him during the thirties. He had felt himself part of history until history turned against itself. One sees this in his admiration of the courage of William Z. Foster; one sees it as he describes the young Russians with whom he travels from London to Leningrad as they give him "a favorable impression of the new Soviet culture"; one sees it in the portraits that line the gallery entitled *To the Finland Station.* It was the human aspirations voiced in Marxism that had captured his imagination in 1931. When he came to reject the authoritarian temper of Marxism, he tried to retain his faith in those aspirations. But he was never to be really successful in finding another home.

3

The Retreat from Politics

> *Liberalism is that principle of political rights, according to which the public authority, in spite of being all-powerful, limits itself and attempts, even at its own expense, to leave room in the States over which it rules for those to live who neither think nor feel as it does, that is to say as do the stronger, the majority. Liberalism—it is well to recall this to-day—is the supreme form of generosity; it is the right which the majority concedes to minorities and hence it is the noblest cry that has ever resounded in this planet.*
>
> From Ortega y Gasset's *The Revolt of the Masses*

To a generation now engaged in the task of remythicizing the 1930s, the forties are bound to present themselves as one of the drabber decades in American life. It is with a strange inability to believe, an emotion approaching shock, that one remembers that the fate of Western man hung in the balance during the first half of that decade which witnessed the single most savage and sustained attack upon civilization ever known. But because the rebirth of the thirties has been a rebirth as much of sentiment as of critical judgment, the fate of the forties (and who does not find himself tired of these generational peregrinations that almost seem compulsive when one is writing about the American intellectual scene?) has been, at least for the time being, settled rather decisively. It was a crude decade, deserving of the adjectives "low" and "dishonest" which Auden gave its predecessor. In writing about it, critics seem curiously oblivious to the fact of the Second World War.

Wilson, too, was more or less indifferent to the war, at least until its closing months when he left for Europe to write his "Sketches Among the Ruins of Italy, Greece and England" for the *New Yorker*. His indifference was purposeful. He insisted that the war was no more than a struggle between rival technological powers equally devoid of any meaning other than what he was later to call "the voracity of the sea slug." However admirable such a refusal to breach the artist's independence may have been, his work during the entire decade suffered from rootlessness and lack of focus. There is a historical, dislocation that seems to grow out of *To the Finland Station*, a sense that, having been betrayed by history once, the writer can do little more than to seek to simplify history. His case has a great deal in common with the depreciation of artistic focus that one finds in Dos Passos once he took leave of the myth of the dialectic for the myth of Jeffersonian America.

Classics and Commercials does for Wilson's work in the forties what *The Shores of Light* does for his work in the twenties and thirties: it serves as a literary chronicle. But what it most effectively chronicles is the dissolution of Wilson's own criticism. The pervasive tone of the collection is elegiac; it is filled with "self-doubt" and a greater fear of "public disapproval" than a writer as independent and courageous as Wilson cared to live with; one discovers a sense of groping, a critical confusion, and this on the part of a writer who had once seemed so certain in his judgments but who now was struggling to tie perceptions together, to come through with something more than his integrity intact. Wilson seems to have deliberately turned away from political journalism in order to concentrate on criticism, reviewing and *Memoirs of Hecate County*, as if he were reacting to a kind of spiritual bankruptcy that set in after the completion of his great study of socialism. The isolation that he chose was a courageous and perhaps necessary gesture for one who believed that the war represented little more than "the irresistable instinct of power to expand itself." But it had the unfortunate result of making him appear crabbed, alienated not merely from the country and the times but, paradoxically enough, from the very creative vision which he so bitterly defended in a famous attack on Archibald MacLeish.

It is not merely that in *Classics and Commercials* one loses the anticipation of the new that makes *The Shores of Light* perhaps the best introduction we have to the literary tone of the years between 1922 and 1938; one loses, too, the idea that criticism and reviewing are intellectually valid functions. It is never quite clear why Wilson devoted himself so ardently to the task of destroying the reputations of writers who were essentially without reputation. Why all of these pages attacking Louis Bromfield, Anya Seton, Somerset Maugham, Kay Boyle, and detective stories? His method of reviewing had not changed. What seems to have changed for the duration of the war was his belief in the vitality of literature itself. He is successful in demolishing best sellers and detective stories, but the more he demands allegiance to the imaginative act the less capable he is of dealing with that act critically. He does not make us feel that literature can provide the salvation of civilization for which he calls. Nor can he be excused on the basis of a lack of subject matter. What more opportune time for a major critic to have written about Thomas Mann than in the forties? But Wilson met the publication of *Dr. Faustus* with absolute silence. "Thoughts on Being Bibliographed" is both revealing and guarded and it exhibits that mixture of despondency and querulousness which personified his mood. As the "record of a journalist," it does not satisfy simply because Wilson, a man who has dealt with himself far more honestly than most of his contemporaries, is here far too self-conscious, too intent on summarizing movements which have "run their courses."

It is not wholly fair to judge Wilson on the pieces in *Classics and Commercials*. But when one turns to the two books of criticism which he published in 1941, *The Boys in the Back Room* and *The Wound and the Bow*, the story is not very different. *The Boys in the Back Room* is as insignificant as it is short; it is the only one of Wilson's books in which the subject matter is trivial. And it is the only one of Wilson's books in which even the prose seems hurried. Wilson discusses a group of California novelists whom he rather weakly contends "constitute a sort of group." But the geographical unity which he imposes on James M. Cain, Horace McCoy, Richard Hallas, John O'Hara, William Saroyan, Hans Otto Storm, and John Steinbeck is a critical whim rather than a critical insight. Other than an occasionally relevant remark he seems content to do little more than summarize what they have written. And for a critic of Wilson's stature to slap at Saroyan for playing the "unappreciated genius" is like a lion wrestling with a house cat. The only observation that interests a contemporary reader is when Wilson points out Steinbeck's "preoccupation with biology," an idea which has since been expanded by other critics of Steinbeck's work. But when he finishes this short book, the reader can only come to the conclusion that Wilson wrote it simply to announce his emergence from the world of socialism. The book lacks focus; it is a critical journey taken with neither commitment nor real curiosity. And it winds up by slighting the one truly important figure with whom it deals, Nathanael West.

The Wound and the Bow is not so light a book. Wilson here makes extensive use of the kind of Freudian technique he had used in parts of *To the Finland Station*. But in applying this technique to a group of writers, he is ultimately the victim of his book's thesis, "the idea that genius and disease, like strength and mutilation, may be inextricably bound up together." Where the unity of *The Boys in the Back Room* was geographical, here it is psychological. It is almost as dubious a unity, although the essays themselves are by far superior to the hastily sketched notes which make up *The Boys in the Back Room*. Two of these essays, in fact, the long study of Dickens and "The Kipling That Nobody Read," are among the best essays Wilson has written as a critic. In both, he focuses upon certain neglected phases in the career of a well-known writer and he succeeds, in each case, in enabling us to see the writer as we have not seen him before. In the essay on Kipling he succeeds brilliantly, but it is a success which signifies a retreat from a larger involvement, one of the first indications that he is moving away from contemporaneity. He develops a cogent analysis of Kipling's achievement from the starting point of Kipling's "fundamental submissiveness to authority." The analysis of Kipling's childhood and adolescence and the effects they had upon the development of his art, along with the effects of English imperialism and the repressiveness of English class structure are joined in such a way as to make us see Kipling anew without the apologetic tone that T. S. Eliot employed when he wrote about Kipling's verse.

"Dickens: The Two Scrooges" is almost as successful, although the reason Wilson gives for writing the essay, that "Charles Dickens has received . . . the scantiest serious attention from either biographers, scholars, or critics," has since been rectified. But when one considers that it was originally published in 1940, and that it grew out of a seminar Wilson conducted in the summer of 1939 at the University of Chicago, it remains a truly impressive critical achievement. It is an essay which represents Wilson's fusion of the Marxist and Freudian techniques of literary analysis. He was never to discard what he had learned about class from his studies of socialism. With the notable exception of George Orwell, no other English or American critic has understood the centrality of class to the creation of the writer's point of view better than Wilson.[1]

For Wilson, Dickens is not only declassed but is haunted by memories of his own descent into the social hell of Newgate. Wilson never permits himself the indulgence of transforming Dickens into a Marxist; what he does—and what is, of course, far more effective—is to show him as a writer intent on tracing the "anatomy of that society" which Marx himself had set out to destroy. Like Orwell's own essay on Dickens, it is today more interesting for the statement of its perceptions than for its originality. But its blending of individual and class psychology is not only accurate; it is also dramatic. One reads this kind of criticism with a certain suspense.

And yet, the other essays in *The Wound and the Bow,* including the well-known "Hemingway: Gauge of Morale," are inferior to most of the essays in *The Triple Thinkers.* This may be, at least in part, because they are read in the context of the book which makes the reader much too aware of Wilson's thesis. But there is also far too great an element of what Hyman labeled the critic as "translator" in most of these essays. "Uncomfortable Casanova" strikes the reader as too brisk, too easy, and too intent on pigeonholing where it should illuminate. There are moments when in reading these essays we begin to suspect that Wilson is so intent on showing us the wound that he is oblivious to the bow.

Wilson's thesis, his attempt to tie together the six preceding essays, is presented in the concluding essay, "Philoctetes: The Wound and the Bow"; here the artist is presented as the possessor of an omnipresent psychic wound as well as the sole possessor of the one weapon capable of curing society of the effects of that wound, his art. But the artist's wound continues to suppurate long after we have concluded the essay, for Wilson's thesis is singularly unconvincing. As an attempt to unify a collection of essays, it leaves the reader wondering whether the disease-creativity metaphorical syndrome was not merely an unwieldly attempt to uncover a substitute for his waning Marxism. In the essays on Kipling and Dickens Wilson succeeds in creating levels of statement about his theme, but these are the only two essays in which he is very convincing. And, one suspects, this in itself testifies to the limitations of the thesis. A more analytic criticism might have led him to test his thesis with other authors than those he chose.

The poetry in *Note-Books of Night,* a collection published in 1942, is interesting because of its painfully autobiographical content. The opening poem, "Night in May," seems to summarize Wilson's mood: "This is the zero hour—all troubles and all blurs—/The will is lulled and falters, the dog desire stirs." The lines seem descriptive of Wilson's mood during the war years, although the poem was actually published for the first time in 1935. A love poem, it joins the pressures of the past to the needs of the present. But the phrase, "the will is lulled and falters," describes Wilson's mood during the war years. And if Wilson is not by temperament a poet, he is still capable of a certain focused satire. The betrayal of the Leninist ideal is given us in "Chorus of Stalin's Yes-Men." In "The Playwright in Paradise," Hollywood, traditionally one of Wilson's bêtes noires, is attacked very humorously. (Wilson is better at satirizing institutions than people: "The Omelet of A. MacLeish" is cruel, but it does not really work because Wilson never quite manages to make MacLeish the personification of the writer who accommodates himself to whichever political belief is currently in fashion.)

But the best of these poems embrace an elegiac tone which extends not merely to individuals but to a world now breaking apart. "On Editing Scott Fitzgerald's Papers" is not only a deeply moving expression of personal grief at the death of a friend; it is a poem which, in many respects, remains the psychological if not literary summit of all that Wilson wrote and it speaks of the wrecked careers and lives of his generation, of talents washed up on the shore, of men dead before they could renew their promise.

And I, your scraps and sketches sifting yet,
Can never thus revive one sapphire jet,
However close I look, however late,
But only spell and point and punctuate.

The awareness of death, certainly not new to Wilson's work, is in these poems threatening and immediate. To be cut off from one's political faith and one's country is difficult enough, but to be cut off from one's talent before it has succeeded in endowing promise with permanence is the greatest of all threats.

Memoirs of Hecate County was published in 1946 and when it was reissued thirteen years later Wilson spoke of it as "my favorite among my books." At this point, it is difficult to discover whether he likes it because of its virtues or because it is the book which, in the very totality of its suburban desperation, speaks of the successful stand he made against chaos, disintegration, and the temptation of surrender. It can best be read as a conscious act of defiance, one of those embarrassingly intimate books in which the artist stands himself against the world by attempting an absolute honesty. Flaubert is one master; Proust and James others; Freud yet a fourth. And yet, it is a curiously unmodern work of fiction. Unlike the writing in *I Thought of Daisy*, the writing in these fictionalized *Memoirs* is distinctly nineteenth century in tone and texture. So apparent is his desire to stamp the book with his honesty that it almost seems as if Wilson deliberately closed his mind to the possibilities inherent in the very techniques he had once brought to public attention in *Axel's Castle*.

The book consists of five stories and a short novel, "The Princess With the Golden Hair," all of them narrated by the protagonist, an art historian obviously modeled upon Wilson himself. The best of the stories, "Ellen Terhune," is most effective for the way in which it evokes a certain fin-de-siècle atmosphere and it reminds the reader, in some of its effects, of Oscar Wilde's *The Picture of Dorian Gray*. The story illustrates the extent to which Wilson's power as a writer of fiction had been tied to his power to resist, to say no to a world that threatened to swallow him, to protect those qualities of imagination, morality, and integrity which were to seem as old-fashioned, in the America that emerged from the Second World War, as the wagon trains in which nineteenth-century Americans confronted the physical challenge of a continent as they pursued a dream which, in the final pages of these *Memoirs*, has long since been buried in the past.

> It was not really the new country any more; it was the old country: we had passed it in history; and the loves and achievements of our youth had all taken place elsewhere.

But Wilson is so intent on summarizing the experience of his generation in the person of his narrator that the dramatic line of the book is always slipping away from us in a peculiarly didactic vision of the nation in search of itself confronted by a narrator in search of the nation. The book's weakness then becomes apparent. For in seeking personal explanation, Wilson somehow managed to force himself away from what was really central about America. The events in the book take place in the years between the First World War and the entrance of the United States into the Second World War; in short, they span both the times and the conflicts through which Wilson had lived since his emergence on the literary scene. The narrator, who seeks salvation in the pursuit of his craft as an art critic, is finally overwhelmed by an America which has little use for the art of an Ellen Terhune, which has, in fact, little use for anything that is honest. For this is a world of high culture which resembles the world of high finance, except that it does not admit what it is even to itself; its hypocrisy will not permit it to see the extent to which it has become the prisoner of the specious commercialism which destroys opportunity in America. Wilson is writing about his own long descent from centrality in American intellectual life; little more than ten years after *Memoirs of Hecate County* was published, he could ask, with a certain tone of self-satisfaction, "Am I, then, in a pocket of the past?"

But the country about which he is writing in these *Memoirs* is simply not our country. It may provide us with an excellent description of what the depression meant to America's upper-middle class and its sycophants, but this does not make it our America either. Wilson condemns without really wanting to understand the country. He is so out of sympathy with his characters that he becomes out of touch with his nation. And since the nation is what he wishes to interest the reader in, what he has written is a book that fascinates the reader without engaging him. The narrator leaves us with the strange sense that he has passed the country by in the very intensity of his desire to paint it for us. The moral corruption and suburban lifelessness of Hecate County are effectively done, but if Wilson intended Hecate County as a metaphorical landscape for modern America, and it is evident that he did, then he does not really succeed. The book's final passage, with its tributary echoes of *The Great Gatsby*, simply does not grow out of its artistic core. There is something hauntingly unreal about this America. We can believe that the narrator and his girl friend discover "the fears and suffocations, the drugged energies, of Hecate County" when they journey west; we can believe in the world of these high-powered publishers and their art-critic victims, for the Milhollands and the sinister duo, Mr. and Mrs. Blackburn, have their prototypes in the Bennett Cerfs and the Luces; and although the working class is seen from the outside looking in, as if the narrator were a rich boy wandering in a slum in search of excitement, we can even believe in—or at least accept—his struggle to enter a life beyond the confines of Hecate County. We can believe all of this, but we cannot, finally, accept his America as ours. For while the metaphor is stated, it is never locked in our consciousness as great metaphors inevitably are.

But if Wilson paid a price for writing it, *Memoirs of Hecate County* is still a book which possesses some very substantial virtues. It is solid and thorough; it is insightful in its exploration of the world of Hecate County; few American novels surpass it in the way in which it depicts the undermining of the values of an older America, the collapse of moral and intellectual standards of behavior, and the moral decline which seized the "better Americans" during the depression. It has long since been an intellectual cliché that American manners and mores are established not by the upper but by the middle class, and a European who has difficulty understanding this might do worse than to read *Memoirs of Hecate County.*

It is Wilson's only work of fiction in which the descriptive power of the writing is up to the level of *The American Jitters.*[2] And while it lacks a dramatic focus, it is rarely dull. Like Nick Carraway in *The Great Gatsby,* the narrator is the eye through whom we see the world of Hecate County unfold. It is the narrator who describes the Machiavellianism of Clarence Latouche in "The Man Who Shot Snapping Turtles," a prelude for what is to follow; it is he who, in "Ellen Terhune," tries to work his way back into that "atmosphere which had first been established at the beginning of the eighties" by imagining himself into the world of the creative artist; it is he who, through "Glimpses of Wilbur Flick," traces the decline of a generation from 1912—the year Wilson himself entered Princeton—to the late 1930s, by which time Wilbur Flick has run through a number of wives, a great deal of money, drugs, fascism, alcohol, sanitariums, the WPA, and the standard flirtation with communism which seemed required of those who possessed neither courage nor independence but a modicum of talent; in "The Princess With the Golden Hair," it is the narrator who finds himself caught between two women who represent two worlds, one the vitiated fantasized medievalism of the educated middle class ensnared in its own sexual neuroses, the other a far less convincing girl from the working class (another representative of the "common life," equipped, like Daisy, with a "clear little sense of things" and an "appetite for love" which are "the true sanction for life") ensnared by physical sickness and poverty; and it is the narrator who not only witnesses but surrenders to the world of commercialized publishing scathingly depicted in the final two stories, "The Milhollands and Their Damned Soul" and "Mr. and Mrs.

Blackburn at Home," as he surrenders his integrity and his desire to do something worthwhile for the satisfaction of money and of being "at home" with the Blackburns.

Memoirs of Hecate County was, one suspects, Wilson's last attempt to come to terms with this America and with the world in which he was living. Having ignored the war intentionally until its end, having forced himself into an isolation not of place but of the style of his life and thought, he was to content himself after *Europe Without Baedeker* with engaging an enemy which increasingly seemed modernity itself. The pacifistic sentiment which Wilson apparently took from his own experience of the First World War had served him well; but in his stubborn insistence that the Second World War was no more than a power struggle between rival technologies with essentially similar aims, he reduced an immense tragedy to a personal betrayal. The narrator of *Memoirs of Hecate County* gives himself to the world of power and money. If the narrator is a projection of what Wilson thought he himself might have become had he succumbed to the pressures plaguing American intellectuals in the years between the wars, then the course the real-life Wilson chose to follow becomes even more understandable. But for all of that, it produced a constriction of his sympathies.

When Wilson departed for Europe as the war drew to its close in the spring of 1945, he was, from all indications, an embittered human being. Until this point, his chief, if not only, concern with the war had been to protect the life of mind and imagination.

Europe Without Baedeker, the result of that journey, was originally undertaken on assignment for the *New Yorker.* As a book, it was first published in 1947 and was reissued, along with *Notes from a European Diary: 1963–1964,* nineteen years later. Where the depression and its effects dominated his work from 1929 to the publication of *To the Finland Station* in 1940, this was his first sustained attempt to look at the war. Arriving in Europe at the time of its greatest misery, he confronted the physical and emotional nadir of its people with a pervasive sense of bittnerness and that absence of compassion that made *The American Jitters* so human and so memorable a document.

The prose of the book is what first disturbs the reader. It is still characteristically precise, the work of a writer who has long since settled all problems of style. But Wilson's growing predilection for biological metaphors leaves the reader very uncomfortable. The war-ravaged Neapolitans "have as little relation to people as small octopi, crabs and molluscs brought in by the marine tide." The metaphor is graphically effective, but it produces in the reader the idea that seeing the war at first-hand dehumanized the writer. Unlike his reaction to the people he confronted on his journey through America in 1931, he is here out of sympathy, resentful at being called upon to bear witness to this more devastating brutality. Perhaps this simply testifies to the fact that the suffering he was now witnessing was simply too immense to be scaled down to recognizably human dimensions, that it was impossible for him, in the closing days of the war, to feel anything much greater than exhaustion. Wilson had apparently passed the point beyond which strain on a writer's sympathies is creative. And he is so lacking in sympathy for this Europe that he is content to lecture it by "plugging the virtues of the United States." In fairness to Wilson, it should be noted that when the book was republished in 1966 he noted such "plugging" with embarrassment.

But throughout the book, we are constantly being reminded of how Wilson has come from a superior to an inferior civilization: "the United States at the present time is politically more advanced than any other part of the world." His own generation had lived to see "in the last fifty years a revival of the democratic creativeness which presided at the birth of the Republic and flourished up through the Civil War." And it is the United States in which "the real English social revolution occurred," for "the United States stands to England in the relation of England's own modern history, as if the first French Republic had been detached and set up in another country, where it was able to prosper in a material way far more than it could have done at home." One finds a vision of American innocence which, if not as bucolic as de Crèvecoeur's, seethes with anguish at the spectacle of English propaganda working "again and again on inexperienced and unsuspicious Americans."

The United States is not only a more innocent but a morally superior civilization, especially when measured against the decline of English civilization. England remains Wilson's bête noire, as it was in *Travels in Two Democracies*. In this book, Shakespeare seems an even longer time ago. The Englishmen he depicts remind one of Orwell's proles: they have picked up such banal American habits as gum-chewing, but they have not learned to accept that class fluidity which mitigates against the effect of banality in America. One of the book's peculiarities is that Wilson should feel so obviously at home in London and yet remain so antipathetic to the British themselves. There are moments when the reader feels that Wilson believes that English destitution is something which the British have brought upon themselves, as if he were a vengeful Puritan divine for whom depicting war-torn London as the visible manifestation of God's will brought great satisfaction. There is something that borders on the obscene in his description of soldiers in London "immersed like amoebas in the swampy backwater of England," for he seems intent on ignoring what they and their nation have just come through.

In the same way, the discussion of prostitution in Naples, Rome, and London reflects the attenuation of his sympathies. At first, as we witness his haggling with women, we are struck by the thought that prostitution has become the most human aspect of life in this soul-shredded continent. The prostitutes are recognizably human—they laugh, drink, and gossip, and they comprise one of the few identifiable pictures of possibility in this world, even if it is a possibility limited to being harbingers living off the decay. But the reader is soon disturbed by Wilson's tireless descriptions of what these women look like, how they approach him, and how he confronts them. The novelist here fails and the journalist is not sure of his purpose. The result is that all of these sexual encounters simply add up to one more dehumanized element in a book composed of dehumanized elements. The actual encounters with the prostitutes, in our self-consciously liberated age, seem stale and uneventful. In "The Princess With the Golden Hair," Wilson tried to bring to sexuality the kind of artistic significance that one finds in Proust or in Lawrence. His failure there was a failure of art: he lacks the sexual mystique of Lawrence, just as he lacks the monumental artistry that enabled Proust to see in "the impossibility of ideal romantic love"—and it is significant that the words are Wilson's own—"the break-up of a whole emotional idealism." But in *Europe Without Baedker*, the sexual emptiness is merely another reflection of Wilson's lack of empathy with his subject matter. These encounters merely illustrate that "the respect for human life in itself has . . . largely disappeared in the course of this last war." But there is little in the book, other than a half-hearted invoking of the old prop of democratic socialism along with a controlled eugenics program designed to produce "better human beings," which resurrects one's respect for human life.

All that Wilson is willing to give us are a few isolated portraits of men who are still striving for excellence in the midst of desolation. The Greek archeologist who never thinks "about anything but Minoan ruins" earns Wilson's respect because he has "stuck to his interests and managed to survive and pursue them through the disasters of recent years." But is this enough to preserve civilization? And is it as admirable as Wilson seems to think? The portraits of Santayana, of Malraux, of Silone, and of Kemp Smith, Wilson's former teacher at Princeton, are fragments shored up against the ruins. From the shelter of his convent in Rome, Santayana seeks to impose order and discipline on a world which, one feels, he would scarcely recognize, let alone concern himself with, were he to walk outside its walls. He is intended to serve as a symbol of rationality and humanism in a world strikingly devoid of both. Malraux and Silone, on the other hand, have come through the same wave of Marxism which once bore Wilson, too. In writing about them, he is, one feels, writing about himself. Deeply committed to literary values, they still "have never lost their hold on the social developments, larger and more fundamental, that lie behind national conflicts." But for Wilson, such "social developments" are, from this point on, to become increasingly internalized. Even at the height of his Marxism, Wilson had been uncomfortable with its religious guises. For theology, he has substituted a conception of civilization. And in reading *Europe Without Baedeker*, especially after the economic revival of those cities which he here depicts like so many dried-out grapes waiting to be plucked from the vine, one begins to understand why the book's tone is so bitter. Wilson's journey to the heart of the war left him with little to fall back on as far as civilization was concerned. The book is virtually a farewell to civilization.

And it is here that Wilson succeeds, almost in spite of himself. For the ruins of this Europe will not show up in some future Baedeker, like the ruins of past civilizations. These ruins are total, and yet they are local and individual, too. They testify to the absence of personality and the destruction of individualism in the very cradle of Western culture. It is not by accident that Wilson chose Rome, Athens, and London as the geographic circumference of his journey. The cities are different, but they speak of a collective dissolution. Rome even remains comparatively attractive for him, even if its incredible poverty has "converted [it] into one great brothel." But with whatever ancient monuments have survived intact to be spread like fertilizer across the postwar growth of Europe, the reality that we confront is the reality of death itself. The puritan has retraced his steps, only to find himself revolted by a world in which "we all seem stewing like lumps of flesh and fat in a cheap but turbid soup that washes through the winding channels like the bilge of a Venetian canal." The book might have come from a Johnathan Edwards miraculously resurrected to be thrust down into the charnel house of Europe at the close of the war. The impression of decay is so vivid, the disgust so deep-rooted, and the sense of potential violation at the hands of what passes for humanity in this Europe so intensely felt by the author that it is no wonder that, when the book was republished in 1966, Wilson did not seem particularly conscious of the potential for irony which he now possessed. He is not really interested in swinging London, in De Gaulle's Paris or in Fellini's Rome.[3] And no wonder. For it is in his own disgust with European decay that the book redeems itself. His very lack of sympathy, his immense anguish at all this squalor, and his unorthodox view of the war and its causes are all to the advantage of the puritan. One is reminded of Pound's Mauberley, for the Europe which Wilson here describes is struggling to stay alive—and it is oblivious to its past except insofar as that past can be merchandised, impatient with any dignity which does not translate itself into immediate profit, fetid in its lumpishness, and frightened of being swallowed up by the twin giants of the Soviet Union and the United States.

Wilson produced his studies of the Zuñi and Haitian cultures, which were later incorporated into *Red, Black, Blond and Olive*, in the late forties, but *Europe Without Baedeker* marks the end of his participation in the decade's intellectual life. It was, as we have seen, a limited participation. Nor was the decade's passing a cause for regret as far as he was concerned. Despite his great productivity, he reminds one of an isolated hungry animal during these years, slouching from side to side in a cage too small to contain him. There is, perhaps, no one to fault for this. The world could not be expected to nurse his cuts and bruises when it had so many of them itself, nor could Wilson give up that which he increasingly came to depend upon, his sometimes truculent independence, in order to accept an unacceptable world. By definition, the writer is an outsider. But when he isolates himself so totally, as Wilson was tempted to do during these years, his work itself proves to be the loser.

Looking back on these years with the knowledge of what was to follow, one can only regret that the dominant tone of Wilson's work was so elegiac. It was then that he apparently conceived of the personal past as something toward which he could gravitate. Were Wilson the kind of writer who, like Proust, could re-create the past through enmeshing himself totally in its intricacies, then literature itself would have been the beneficiary. But this did not prove to be the case. Neither as a critic nor as an essayist was he ever to recapture the past successfully. In the forties, he seems to have divorced himself from the culture in which he lived. Had this led to the kind of questioning of the quality of national life and aims that one finds in *The American Jitters,* it would have been all to the good. Instead, it put him in a position which, at the time of his greatest fame and admiration, the late fifties and early sixties, increasingly exposed him to the charge—usually made by younger critics—of having turned his back on the country and the culture. The protest with which Wilson announced his momentary return to the kind of problems which had disturbed him so much in the thirties, *The Cold War and the Income Tax,* is an incredibly depressing book for a man who was once among the country's most astute social critics to have written.

The forties were also the years during which Wilson's reputation reached its nadir. At the present moment, the extent to which he was affected by this cannot be known, but it is difficult to believe anything other than that the effect must have been considerable. He had been the acknowledged leader of the independent Left intellectuals, praised by writers as opposite in temperament as F. O. Matthiessen and Sherwood Anderson. He had stood at the very center of American intellectual life. But now he found both his work and his reputation under attack, a process which culminated in Stanley Edgar Hyman's dismissal of him as a critical "popularizer" whose reputation ultimately rested on his ability to practice a kind of critical "translation." [4]

I do not mean to suggest that Wilson has ever been unduly concerned with his popularity or with his position in American cultural history, but it does seem only natural that he should have welcomed the decade's passing. He certainly had little reason to regret it. In the elegiac tone so characteristic of his writing during these years, in the deaths of such friends and contemporaries as John Peale Bishop and F. Scott Fitzgerald, and in a war which seemed to him senseless and insane, there must have been moments when he sensed the futility of that imaginative vitality to which he clung so desperately. To be out of fashion is not the worst of fates, but to be trapped in a time not of one's choosing at the very moment that one is out of fashion can be extremely taxing on a writer's creative abilities. It is this, I believe, which describes Wilson's situation as the forties came to its nuclear-haunted end.

4

Home As Found

I do not conceive Socialist policy as tied to any particular theory, but to a faith. The more Socialist theories claim to be "scientific," the more transitory they are; but Socialist values are permanent. The distinction between theories and values is not sufficiently recognized but it is fundamental. On a group of theories one can found a school; but on a group of values one can found a culture, a civilization, a new way of living together among men.

From Silone's *The God That Failed*

So we beat on, boats against the current, borne back ceaselessly into the past.

From Fitzgerald's *The Great Gatsby*

In 1927, Charles and Mary Beard could express faith in the potential for change that the intellectual brings to his culture with the following sentence: "The history of a civilization, if intelligently conceived, may be an instrument of civilization." This, in fact, is the opening sentence of their classic, *The Rise of American Civilization.* But in our own, less sanguine, times, one might create a reverse syllogism by writing, "The history of an intellectual, if honestly told, may extend an individual's sense of limitation to the civilization itself." This would certainly offer a better explanation of the course Wilson seems to have chosen. During the last two decades, especially since the publication of *The Shores of Light* in 1952, Wilson has increasingly come to resemble a kind of literary Buddha in the process of being hallowed by the national culture. But just as he once made of his integrity a defiance of that culture, so he now seems to be creating literary capital out of his distant but Augustan presence rather than from his work. Perhaps this is simply to say that Wilson is more contemporary than he cares to admit. We live during a time when the writer and actor are virtually indistinguishable; increasingly, the writer's image becomes more important than the writer's work.

If *The Shores of Light* provides us with a cultural graph on which we can read the major movements of the literary consciousness of the twenties and thirties, and if *Classics and Commercials* represents Wilson's confusion and struggle during the forties, then all that one can say of his most recent collection, *The Bit Between My Teeth,* is that it is so peripheral to the main streams of literary development in our time that to call it a "literary chronicle of 1950–1965" is incredibly misleading. It is, as a matter of fact, the work of a man eminently satisfied with that "pocket of the past" which he has staked out as his private domain.

The fact that Wilson is no longer interested in the contemporary development of literature is possibly not to be regretted. Is it, one wonders, of any major consequence that Wilson, in his sixties and seventies, did not choose to write about Mailer or Genet? One wonders whether any critic writing today can be a discoverer as Wilson was in the twenties and thirties. Where once the academy ignored all post-Tennysonian signs of life, it is guilty today of gobbling up the contemporary before it can even establish its presence. *Axel's Castle* was written about a recognizably avant-garde literature, but no avant-garde can develop today, for it is immediately swallowed up by the universities and by the mass media. Wilson fought for the contemporary when to do so was to fight a war. That war has been won, perhaps too decisively. Had it succeeded in doing what Wilson intended it to do, our culture would have needed *Patriotic Gore* immeasureably more than it needed another book, no matter how good, dissecting angst in contemporary fiction.

Over the past twenty years, Wilson has increasingly come to focus on himself, an act which, in part, may explain his limitations as a critic. In a long review of *The Bit Between My Teeth,* Richard Gilman described it as the product of an individual who "has become increasingly detached from the central life of culture in this country, a life he once helped shape and color." Never before had Wilson seemed so self-consciously isolated. Pound's persona may be helpful for the poet, but one wonders about its usefulness for the critic. Even the structure of *The Bit Between My Teeth,* which opens with "A Modest Self-Tribute" and concludes with an appreciation of Mario Praz, contains no real frame for these disparate pieces, so many of them long and even tedious, so many of them fugitive. Wilson had covered much of this ground before, and he had covered it so much better. The tone of his writing remains eulogistic to a fault. He returns to writers and problems which fascinated him in the twenties and thirties—Fitzgerald, Shaw, Mencken, Cabell, Malraux, Auden, Eliot are all once again present—but he does not really return to them as a critic. There is, one sees, impatience with criticism itself. One wonders what the Wilson who wrote *Axel's Castle* would have made of the material scattered through the two essays on de Sade, the two essays on Mario Praz, and the long essay on Swinburne. Here they possess no connection; in earlier times, Wilson might have equaled *The Romantic Agony.* The resurrection of the reputations of George Ade, Cabell, and Swinburne is merely personal; as a result, none of these essays are convincing. In fact, when Wilson attempts here to reassess a writer whose reputation is in decline, he is generally unconvincing. It is difficult to agree that Max Beerbohm has "endured," even if one is charmed by the picture of him that Wilson draws.

There is a confusion in *The Bit Between My Teeth* which reflects an increasing tendency to substitute the morality of a work of art, or even the conditions under which it was created, for the work of art itself. One of the few pieces in this collection which derives from that "moral force" to which he committed himself when he moved closer and closer to the world of his fathers is " 'Miss Buttle' and 'Mr. Eliot.' " In this case, a bad satire of Eliot had offered Wilson a new way into old wars. Recognizing Eliot's unquestioned poetic genius, he very coolly dissects Eliot's deadening personal despair as it assumes the form of Eliotic Christianity which grew so tiresome as one encountered it in graduate schools of English in the 1950s. Here we find an Eliot who, despite his great success, is still similar to the Eliot we had met in *Axel's Castle;* clerical, rather arid, a man whose anti-Semitism is not merely a whim but a severe restriction on his intelligence and sensibility, an individual whose political thinking is the most prosaic nonsense, and a writer whose critical pontificating has given sanction to many of the less fortunate tendencies of modern criticism. And yet, at other times, Wilson is himself incapable of perceiving the work of art. Eliot's Christianity is vestigial and artificial, but is the city for the soul which Pasternak constructed out of Czarist Russia any less vestigial or artificial? In the one case, analysis spurred by an old anger and impatience; in the other, Wilson's passion for the moral act, the artistic act of defiance. *Dr. Zhivago* may be "a great act of faith in art and the human spirit" directed against intellectual charlatanry. But declamation is not criticism and merely to assume that the novel is "one of the great events in man's literary and moral history" does not make it a major novel. In reading the two long essays that Wilson devoted to *Zhivago* and its creator, one is scarcely aware that Zhivago's Russia has its institutionalized pogroms, its anachronistic religion, its obsessive piety, its feudal relationships, its perverted sense of justice, much of it invoked in the name of that same Christianity which Wilson so intelligently dissects in Eliot.

Wilson tries to make his taste ours in *The Bit Between My Teeth.* He succeeds best in the pieces on Eliot and de Sade, neither one of whom can be taken quite so seriously after this. He fails where his taste seems peculiarly self-indulgent, such as in the essays on Swinburne and Cabell. On the whole, however, what is most disturbing is how irrelevant his taste now seems. One simply expects more. And the collection does not even include the best of all the critical essays Wilson wrote during the period covered by this "literary chronicle," "Turgenev and the Life-Giving Drop."[1] Here we once again find the Wilson who set about to learn Russian in order to read Lenin in the original. Few American critics possess the kind of acquaintance with non-English literatures which enable one to write a sentence such as the following:

> He had been able to learn from Pushkin, whom he took for his master, the trick of evading the censorship by telling the story in such a way as to make it convey its moral without any explicit statement, and he was the first Western writer of fiction to perfect the modern art of implying social criticism through a narrative that is presented objectively, organized economically, and beautifully polished in style.

This time in isolation rather than as part of a thesis, the psychoanalytic technique of *The Wound and the Bow* is employed to illuminate a writer, an age, and a culture. Turgenev's life and work are made synonymous with a Russia whose appeal lies in its ability to produce men like Turgenev and Belinsky. In its blending of biography and literary criticism, the essay points back to *Axel's Castle* and forward to *Patriotic Gore*.

But it is not as a literary critic that Wilson presents himself after the publication of *Europe Without Baedeker*. If one desires to create a world at whose center he himself stands, then the limitations of literary criticism are obvious. This desire helps to explain both the tone of the criticism Wilson did write, the wistful desire to recapture the past, and the almost marginal role criticism came to play in his idea of what he was as a writer. His best work in the fifties is in neither political journalism, which he virtually deserted after *Europe Without Baedeker*, or in literary criticism but rather in his personal and historical essays which attempt a kind of cultural summation; it is the desire to look at himself as an individual who embodies a culture that is dying which produces the tone of his work. And this tone is as evident in his essays about his family as it is in *Patriotic Gore*, the book, which, one suspects, he would choose as a summation of self.

To be a patrician is to accept a fate and Wilson's acceptance of the fate of the patrician has apparently grown out of his lack of comfort with the general drift of life in our world. In "The Author at Sixty," the essay which concludes *A Piece of My Mind*, Wilson begins with the theme of personal isolation—and it is this theme which dominates his work after the publication of *Europe Without Baedeker*. "I have lately been coming to feel that, as an American, I am more or less in the eighteenth century—or, at any rate, not much later than the early nineteenth." The essay itself, the conclusion to an intellectual ramble in which Wilson offers us his thoughts about religion, the United States, Europe, Russia, war, the Jews, education, science, and sex, is not so much concerned with Wilson as it is with his father. It is a remarkably skillful piece of writing, a tour de force that manages to localize the conflicts produced by the one hundred years of American history spanned by Wilson and his father in the author's own family. The struggle between personal and historical forces shape the portrait of an old-fashioned American, a morphological contemporary of Jefferson and the elder John Adams, caught against his will in the flaccidity of our postwar twentieth century. The continuity of moral and cultural tradition, the ceaseless quest for integrity, the demands which one is entitled to make upon himself—all are now seen as the harvest of that "moral force" which his father, above all others, willed to him. And it is this force, rather than any intellectual sustenance, which has enabled him to see his way through the endless crises of modern life. The difficulties facing the American who does not believe that he belongs to the country depicted between the covers of *Life* magazine are traced to the acquisitive pressures that erupted in the country after the Civil War, when the older ethic of New York farmers and New England merchants—created and subscribed to by an America that was removed from Europe by more than distance—was engulfed by the rapacity of the Goulds, the Rockefellers, the Carnegies. One is reminded of how strong a factor Wilson's dislike of American business acquisitiveness was in his move toward the Left in the early thirties. Post-Civil War America had come to haunt him and there is a sense in which one can say that *Patriotic Gore* is more the work of his father than of Wilson. For his father, an individual for whom allegiance to one's own intelligence and morality was the moral axis of existence, was to find himself a high-priced subservient to the rapacious captains of industry.

> The period after the Civil War—both banal in a bourgeois way and fantastic with gigantic fortunes—was a difficult one for Americans brought up in the old traditions: the generation of my father and uncles.

The breakdown of this "old tradition" led to his father's lack of objectives in life." And certainly the record of Wilson's father and of his father's generation is among the saddest of all chapters in American history. Rarely had so much talent been devastated by a corruption for which their past and their training alike simply had not prepared them; rarely had gifted men been broken so thoroughly by social pressures they could not understand. It is these very same pressures which have forced Wilson back to meditate on the past, to reflect upon the potential of the human spirit in the rural retreat of Talcottville, New York, or in the summer resort of Wellfleet, Massachusetts, each town like a symbolic emblem out of Hawthorne in the structure it imparts to Wilson's world. The Civil War came to haunt him because it destroyed the "old tradition," and, in destroying it, destroyed the world of his father, too. The war killed the order and stability which Wilson's family represented.

For the fifteen years between the publication of *Europe Without Baedeker* and *Patriotic Gore*, Wilson was to examine the history and literature of the Civil War.[2] It was, one senses, virtually a personal crusade, a return to some symbolic Jerusalem that had haunted him for a major part of his adult life. Although he chose to look at the war as his primary example of human voracity, there seems to be little doubt that the war came to play for him a role remarkably similar to what the crucifixion is to the Christian: the central observable historical phenomenon to which all else—all explanations, all theories, all meaningful moral actions—are subservient. And the fact is that he succeeds in endowing the Civil War with extraordinary metaphorical power, one that suggests a possible explanation (although all historical logic is obviously against this idea) for all of the ills which plague the American soul. Not only did he see the war as marking an end to a culture in which order and stability were derived from the still-vital Puritan ethical tradition, and not only was the war, in the memorable phrase used by the Beards, "the Second American Revolution," it was also the event which chained two unalterably opposed worlds to one another, the world of Wilson's personal and spiritual ancestors—what he called that "heroic, old-fashioned America" which had produced his father, John Jay Chapman, and even Ulysses S. Grant and then, in one way or another, had destroyed them all by making their lives irrelevant to the new world's reality—and modern industrial America, acquisitive, soulless, far more neurotic than what it had willed his father but totally incapable of suffering from a neurosis it could neither see nor feel. The neurotic declines which his father experiences become, as Wilson describes them for us, the price Americans paid for their alienation of the spirit. And it is the

Civil War which ties him to his father, and to his father's world.

> My father's career had its tragic side—he died in his sixty-first year. I have been in some ways more fortunate—I am writing this in my sixty-second. And yet to have got through with honor that period from 1880 to 1920!—even at the expense of the felt-muted door, the lack of first-class companionship, the retreats into sanitariums. I have never been obliged to do anything so difficult. Yet my own generation in America has not had so gay a journey as we expected when we first started out. In repudiating the materialism and the priggishness of the period in which we were born, we thought we should have a free hand to refashion American life as well as to have more fun than our fathers. But we, too, have had our casualties. Too many of my friends are insane or dead or Roman Catholic converts—and some of these among the most gifted; two have committed suicide. I myself had an unexpected breakdown when I was in my middle thirties. It was pointed out to me that I had reached exactly the age at which my father had first passed into the shadow.

"The Author at Sixty" is haunting in the way that only the deepest autobiography can be called haunting. After one has read it, he no longer notices that so much of what has preceded this conclusion is the work of a man essentially out of touch with those very intellectual movements he had once so forcefully charted for American readers. It is only when one returns to the preceding essays that he notices how, for example, the essay on religion offers a remarkably literal interpretation of religion which a contemporary Christian intellectual would simply find unrecognizable. It is, perhaps, an early-nineteenth-century voice which can create an analogy between insanity and Roman Catholicism. But are they analagous? And most of the other pieces in *A Piece of My Mind* seem just as intent on simplifying the world in order to make it understandable. They are the work of a mind which, however brilliant, has simply removed itself from much of what lies open before it.

To read Wilson's work during the fifties is to grow uncomfortably aware that the Civil War cost him not merely a father but a country, too. If we were to apply his own theory of the wound and the bow, then his wound, like Melville's, is isolation from the country of his dreams. It can, of course, be said that Wilson's view of pre–Civil War America is the view of an artist rather than that of a historian; in this sense, its accuracy is not particularly important. But this would also be begging the question of metaphorical validity. We simply know too much about pre–Civil War America to accept all that Wilson tells us. Wilson's fascination with what can only be called the personal past was in evidence long before the 1950s. One can see him writing about it in the Proustian essay, "The Old Stone House," published at the time of Roosevelt's first inaugural; and it is certainly in evidence in his essay on John Jay Chapman included in *The Triple Thinkers*. But in the thirties, the present still possessed vitality and possibility. The importance of the past was then a key to understanding the future. To "refashion American life" was still the writer's job. Whatever failure existed was itself personal and Wilson concluded "The Old Stone House" by confessing that he had "left that early world behind" even if he had never "really succeeded in what was till yesterday the new." The mixture of place and past had always struck a responsive chord in Wilson, but where in the 1930s it was a mixture still imbued with the potential for tragedy, it seems to have increasingly become a refuge, even, one suspects, a shield designed to ward off the complexity of modern existence. To exploit the past as a fixed point of reference is not the same as recapturing it.

But Wilson remains a remarkable writer all through the fifties; the mind is still combative, the reading voluminous. If the criticism begins to disappoint, to move from the sharp impressionism of Wilson's best criticism to what can only be called surprisingly flaccid observations which reflect, more than anything else, the desire to remake the literary world, to right its balance not by judicious assessment but by personal memoir—if this is true, the reporter's eye is still observant. No other American writer, not, certainly, in our century, has desired to be so complete a man of letters. It is not only that Wilson takes pride in being called a "professional"; it is, rather, that he is one of a very small group of writers who, in the quantity of their work and in the quality and range of their interests, have created of their professionalism a way of looking at the world. Wilson—and here we discover his greatest advantage over the more academic critics against whom he is so frequently measured—is a writer whose commitment is total. Even after his retreat, he still brought his intelligence and talent to bear on unusually diverse subjects. Between 1950 and 1967, he published a total of eighteen books. More than half of this material consisted of reprinting and revising work originally published in the years between 1920 and 1950, but the new work reflects his still vivid sense of inquiry. This book has had little to say about Wilson's work as a dramatist because space limitations demand that much of his work be looked at as expendable. But I should note, in this connection, that *The Little Blue Light*, published and produced in 1950, is the best of Wilson's plays, the only one in which we find a resourceful exploitation of a dramatic situation.

With the publication of *The Scrolls from the Dead Sea* in 1955 and *Red, Black, Blond and Olive* in 1956, Wilson continued his investigations of other societies, both geographically and culturally removed from his own. Wilson is instinctively able to do what anthropologists are trained to do, and, because he is a writer with a very thorough idea of what constitutes a civilization, his books about his travels are far more interesting than the work of professional anthropologists. For Wilson, respect for an alien culture is not something which a professional discipline imposes. He comes to each culture with marked receptivity, but it is a receptivity which is never impersonal or defensive; it is, rather, the result of curiosity, a thoroughly old-fashioned curiosity which the contemporary reader welcomes with relief. One does not have to strip his mind of its analytical powers in order to accompany Wilson on a journey to an alien world. *The Scrolls from the Dead Sea,* the essays on "The United States," "Russia," and "The Jews" in *A Piece of My Mind,* and *Red, Black, Blond and Olive* belong together. Not only were all three books published between 1955 and 1956 but the themes they treat were by then endemic to Wilson's thought and pointed toward *Patriotic Gore.* The question of survival, probably derived from the international political cold war that followed the Second World War and the general political repressiveness which reigned in the United States during the later forties and fifties (Wilson had depicted this in a most pessimistic manner in *The Little Blue Light*), is at the heart of all of these books. The problem of the survival of a self within a society apparently accounts for Wilson's growing fascination with the Jews all during these years. In this, he resembles John Jay Chapman, with whose fascination with Jews Wilson obviously empathized. Rootless, intellectual, marked out by a society for which he has mingled contempt and admiration, the Jew became for Wilson a prototype of a particular kind of marginality which intellectuals also experienced. To what does one belong? is the question he asks in these books. Insofar as there is an answer, Wilson binds himself faster and faster to his own perceptions and ideas.

More than any other book he was to write, *Red, Black, Blond and Olive,* which he subtitled *Studies in Four Civilizations,* describes the different claims which non-American cultures made upon him. To the reader familiar with all of Wilson's work, it is not surprising to discover that his quests have been, in large part, motivated by the closest thing to religion which one finds in his life. He depicts himself as an "atavistic Protestant," and what he has to tell us about Zuñi, Haiti, Russia, and Israel are the observations of an individual no longer certain of his patriarchy. The section on the Soviet Union simply reprints the Russian journey of *Travels to Two Democracies,* although, in a characteristically honest fashion, Wilson adds certain bracketed lines which he had suppressed from the original in his attempt "to accommodate my impressions to the ideal of a dream come true." He is now far from that Wilson who had, in first visiting the Soviet Union, supposed that he "was seeing a society which had dispensed with myths, rituals, and symbols." He recognizes that his "respect for the leaders of the October Revolution" had prevented him from accepting the incipient totalitarianism of Soviet society.

> I had not yet gone far enough into Marxism to have noticed the religious element that Marx and Engels had smuggled into their system, under the illusion that they were rejecting religion and had stripped Hegel's dialectic of its idealistic associations.

And he now recognizes that his "yearning for 'Holy Places' is to be seen in my pages on the tomb of Lenin."

The chief source of intellectual tension in the study of these four different societies is the way in which a deeply unreligious man, who, in many respects, reminds us of one of those nineteenth-century Darwinian atheists for whom the loss of God was the chief article of faith, searches in the ruins of myth, in the back alleys and backwaters of alien cultures, to discover how a particular tradition could survive, enmeshed perhaps in its own archaic elements but somehow still able to endow individuals with a belief in their own vital singularity. This is itself a form of religion, the only belief apparently available to an atavistic Protestant.

All of the cultures Wilson examines are founded upon a distinctly mythological element. It is this belief in transcedence which Wilson finds both irritating and inspiring. The conflict he experiences is similar to the kind of war D. H. Lawrence fought against modern industrial society, but Wilson, unlike Lawrence, is not altogether willing to cut himself adrift. He is still too much a child of the Enlightenment. And he still claims, although it is a claim filled with a mocking sense of its own doubt, that what we possess today is better than what has come before; the affirmation is far more muted and qualified than it has been, but it is still there. The cultural coherence that he discovers in Zuñi is admirable, but it is also a source of "exclusiveness and bigotry in relation to the rest of the world." One begins to see that Wilson's moral force is similar to the Quaker's inner light; it is most Protestant insofar as it is individual. The religions for which he feels respect arise from the integrity of the individual conscience rather than from any body of dogma, which undoubtedly accounts for his anti-Catholicism.[3]

Like Hawthorne, Wilson has rejected the beliefs of his ancestors, but he still finds himself trapped by their conflicts. It is not difficult to understand why he is so markedly ill at ease in this world. Despite *Memoirs of Hecate County* and the minute recordings of the European prostitutes in *Europe Without Baedeker,* he resists the sensuous and the primitive. He is curious about that which is pagan, but he is afraid of it, too. In describing the Zuñi Shálako festival, he is aware of the gulf between that civilization which he personally embodies and what he is witnessing. How different his approach is from that of Lawrence can be seen in the following passage:

> For something in me began to fight the Shálako, to reject and repulse its influence just at the moment when it was most compelling. One did not want to rejoin the Zuñis in their primitive Nature cult; and it was hardly worth while for a Protestant to have stripped off the mummeries of Rome in order to fall a victim to an agile young man in a ten-foot mask.

But his refusal to shed the mask of civilization is also the source of the book's compelling interest. Unable to accept a mythology imposed from outside the self, he still finds myth extremely attractive. In his discussions of Zuñi and Haiti, he finds relics of religiosity, throwbacks to the past which still retain some of their former vitality and which may even be preferable to their modern substitutes, such as fascism and communism, now apparently taking over from a dying Christianity. In the end, however, Wilson is fundamentally out of sympathy with the Zuñi; the Shálako is ultimately no more than an aesthetic spectacle. He is a journalist and it has appealed to his instincts for the new, but there is little more that can be said in its favor. By the time he published *Apologies to the Iroquois,* only four years later, he felt himself in much greater sympathy with Indian ceremonials.

The essay on Haiti focuses not merely on voodoo but on the richness and versatility of that fusion of cultures which has created Haitian art and religion. In writing about Haitian literature, Wilson chooses to judge it as he would any other literature; he is intent, first, on discovering the historical circumstances of its development and then on analyzing its aesthetic qualities. His treatment of Haitian literature, in fact, is a model for the way in which white critics can look at the literature of the American Negro today. To argue that such a literature is beyond the literary ken of white critics, as at least a few critics, white and black, have recently argued, is no more than an abdication of the critic's responsibility. Wilson shows us a literature which, at the time he wrote about Haiti, was virtually unknown in the United States but which was rich in material and technique. He treats it with the critical attention and respect it deserves.

But just as the Zuñi Shálako inspired mixed emotions in him, so Haitian culture leaves him uncomfortable. Voodoo is another form of mysticism. And once again we are confronted with the Protestant versus Catholic theme that keeps coming to the surface in his work during the past two decades. In ascribing to his own tradition, the tradition of the Protestant, certain virtues connected to the concrete, the immediate, and the necessary, Wilson contrasts the approach to voodoo of the Methodist Pastor McConnell, who "can allow no compromise with it," to the approach of the Catholic Church, which simply serves to give voodoo a more Westernized guise. His admiration for "the practical side of Protestanism that he [McConnell] so vigorously represents" is a vestige of the Puritan conscience. Like McConnell, he, too, finds "a really fine example of Protestant practice . . . a good deal more impressive than the giving oneself up to God of either the Voodoo-worshipper or the Catholic."

But it is Haiti's sophistication and complexity, the richness of its literature as well as the strong colors of its landscape, which have their greatest appeal for Wilson. And the Haitian character offers him the opportunity to reflect upon the condition of the American Negro.

> On our side, for a native of the United States, a trip to Haiti is immensely instructive. If he has been depressed or discouraged by the Negro community in Harlem as well as by conditions in the South, he may be surprised to discover how stimulating Haiti is. He will note that, though the French were bad masters, they left the Haitians a sounder kind of education than most black Americans have had (though the Haitian Justin Lhérisson gives an example, in his satirical novellette *La Famille des Pitite-Caille,* of a Haitian oration which, for polysyllabic nonsense, sounds exactly like Father Divine). He will try to take account of the theory that the stock of the African tribes from which the Haitians came was superior to that of our Negroes. He may wonder whether the nuisance of segregation may not have kept him from knowing the best of American Negro life. He may

> decide that, however all this may be, our Negroes were particularly unfortunate in having had to share the defeat of the South, in the sense that they were fatally involved in its decadence and humiliation. In the Haitian revolution, the men of color won and were able to enjoy their independence; in our Civil War, they were freed but had to go on living with their ruined masters.

In itself, this paragraph is not particularly important. But it foreshadows that attitude of mind which was to enable Wilson, by the time he came to *Patriotic Gore,* to more or less ignore the Negro as a presence and as a historical force. This is not to argue that the Civil War was an idealistic crusade to end slavery on the part of the North, but also it is not, as we shall see, quite as simple an affair as Wilson makes of it in *Patriotic Gore.* It is not the responsibility of the Protestant to delude himself about the nature of reality.

Wilson's next excursion into an alien culture, *Apologies to the Iroquois,* is a continuation of the line of inquiry of *Red, Black, Blond and Olive.* He is far more sympathetic to the revival of Iroquois consciousness than he was either to the Zuñi Shálako or Haitian voodoo, for he now identifies the revival of Iroquois religion with resistance to centralized authority. Mythology is made pragmatic, and mythology holds the key to the sense of self which can be reinforced through the sense of religious solidarity. The transformation of the individual is what continues to intrigue him. His admiration for the Jews and for Judaism had previously reflected his own need for an ethic which insisted that the individual was competent to meet any moral challenge without a personal savior. Judaism was not trapped by the Christian paradox, while it managed to embrace a conception of ethical salvation through individual integrity. Jacob wrestling unaided with the angel possesses a deep and personal symbolic appeal to the Protestant. And the mythological basis of Iroquois religion and culture does not irritate him as the Zuñi Shálako did. The highly developed sense of self which the Iroquois had managed to perpetuate in the face of the hostility of white soicety elicited his admiration. But in his desire for the spiritual reinforcement which myth provides without a corresponding belief in myth, Wilson seems to be one more victim of the Protestant dilemma.

Apologies to the Iroquois is an admirable piece of journalism, but it leaves the reader disheartened at the sight of Wilson turning virtually everything he touches into a mirror of his discontent with modern life. One empathizes with the call for an end to white arrogance and one cheers the Iroquois on as they join the "world-wide reaction on the part of the non-white races against the meddling and encroachments of the whites." But the reader who is aware of Wilson's past writing is also disturbed by the tedious defense of "personal property," which sounds, at times, as if it might have come from the pen of one of those embittered Roosevelt-haters who dominated the American Right in the 1930s. Is it not, after all, exactly such zoning laws as those Wilson feels are necessary which have helped to create the dreadful Negro ghettos that are leading the United States to the edge of civil chaos? And can one really compare the revival of the scalp lock on the part of young Iroquois men with the revival of the Confederate flag on the part of white middle-class youth "as protests . . . against the prevalent pressures toward acceptance of the mechanical uniformity imposed by industrial civilization?" What is missing from the book is something concrete—a large-scale political movement—on which to build a meaningful protest. There is a striking contradiction in calling for a United States of Europe and, at the same time, embracing the multitude of nationalisms which have seized modern consciousness.

Patriot Gore was the book that Wilson apparently intended as a personal monument which he had carved out of his life and out of his career as an intellectual. Since its publication in 1962, he has published the revised version of *Europe Without Baedeker;* a further revision of *I Thought of Daisy* which reprints, in the same volume, a long short story—"Galahad"—originally published in 1927 and never before reprinted; *The Bit Between My Teeth; The Cold War and the Income Tax; O Canada;* and the first volume of his journal, entitled *A Prelude,* which reprints two stories originally published in *The Undertaker's Garland* and *Travels in Two Democracies.* But even most of the new material that has appeared since *Patriotic Gore* is of interest because it tells us more about Wilson than we formerly knew. Taken together, these books are fragments of an attitude. *Patriotic Gore,* on the other hand, is a testament.

It is not a book to be spoken of dispassionately, for it challenges one's response not only to Wilson but to living in the modern world. The challenge is both structural and intellectual. To assess the book, one must bring to it his own very intimate knowledge of how the struggle which Wilson seized as a subject has not yet resolved itself, that it seems, if anything, to hold out an even bleaker prospect today than it did when this book was published in the early sixties. In his introduction to the book which one critic, in his enthusiasm, was to label "our American Plutarch," Wilson accepts the implications of his own pacifism.

> The unanimity of men at war is like that of a school of fish, which will swerve, simultaneously and apparently without leadership, when the shadow of an enemy appears, or like a sky-darkening flight of grasshoppers, which, also all compelled by one impulse, will descend to consume the crops.

This forms an eloquent conclusion to an equally eloquent introduction, a plea for the recognition of those instincts which drive men to war. Having lived through the first sixty years of this century of total war, Wilson can "no longer . . . take very seriously the professions of 'war aims' that nations make." The eloquence, the passion, the deeply rooted morality which stand behind each word of this introduction are as moving as they are forceful. But there is apparent here, too, that element which ultimately scars the entire work, a desire, already evident in *Europe Without Baedeker*, to force all wars, all conflicts, into the container of the puritan's morality. The perception is too simple; ultimately, it grates against the thesis.

On the whole, the critical reception of *Patriotic Gore* was highly favorable. One suspects that the book created its accolades even before it was published. Critic after critic viewed it more as a moral act than as a book, an act designed to force Americans into what the historian, David Donald, described as a "profound and disturbing reexamination of our intellectual history." But even those critics who saw the book as a moral act were disturbed by the peculiar kind of logic which asked, "In what way, for example, was the fate of Hungary, at the time of its recent rebellion, any worse than the fate of the South at the end of the Civil War?"

One must begin with the fact that Wilson's historical probes are now shaped to suit the purpose of his zoological metaphors. Nations are "sea slugs," each of them as voracious in its appetite for conquest as the other. But does this not finally voice a pacifist plea which employs that very moral relativism which Wilson had once worried about? Are Lenin, Bismarck, and Lincoln really cut from the same cloth, each of them, "through the pressure of the power which he found himself exercising . . . an uncompromising dictator"? And can one really equate Negroes struggling for their rights with Southerners struggling to ward off the encroachments of the federal bureauracy, that gigantic octopus which, in Wilson's recent writing, has taken on the guise of a protean monster at whose feet all the ills of contemporary life can conveniently be laid? To struggle against oppression is different from the struggle to oppress. And this is not changed simply because Wilson finds it possible "to sympathize with both Negroes and whites." And what, finally, can one make of the rather incredible argument which provides psychological justification to South African apartheid because the Boers are still smarting over their defeat by the British in the Boer War.

> They take out their own humiliation on the blacks who are at their mercy, and the whites of the frustrated Confederacy take out theirs on the Negroes among whom they live.

Perhaps this is simply the wound of the artist now extended to blanket entire civilizations, but is this not too expensive a price to pay even for pacifism?

One does not have to argue that the international behavior of the United States has been very much different from the behavior of other nations. But political thinking, as Wilson once knew, can never support an absolute morality, especially when that morality takes the form of a relativism which, in effect, moralizes the moral out of existence. Wilson's predilection to see dictators everywhere could already be seen in his description of Roosevelt's first inauguration. But the differences between Lenin and Roosevelt, like the differences between Lenin and Bismarck and Bismarck and Lincoln, are rather profound; in part, they are the result of the political systems in which each man matured, in part the result of those political alternatives which were open to him. To lump them together on the basis of some overwhelming sense of destiny is an abdication of the intellectual task of the historian.

The introduction suffers from an overwhelmingly simplistic interpretation of history, but it also, unfortunately, sets the tone for the rest of the book. After one has reread *Patriotic Gore*, one wonders whether Wilson ever got over the shock he describes in the introduction when, as a child, he heard a Virginia cousin refer to Lincoln as "a bloody tyrant." One can, of course, argue that the book is not really intended as history, that it is, rather, a kind of morality pageant in which the lives of a number of Americans are linked to that turning point in our history known as the Civil War. But when morality and history are fused, as they are in Plutarch, then one has the right to expect a dangerous myth to be destroyed by truth rather than to be replaced by a different but equally dangerous myth. Wilson's ideas about war and, in particular, his thesis about the Civil War seem no more accurate than what they were intended to replace. It may be that, as he writes, "the minds of nations at war are invariably dominated by myths, which turn the conflict into melodrama and make it possible for each side to feel that it is combatting some form of evil." But to go from this to the assumption that the myth of the debunker is any more valid than the myth of the partisan is to employ a rather wishful logic. It may, at certain times, be more necessary. But that is all.

Wilson is so attracted to the kind of historical view from above which he voices that he can be said to be the prisoner of that view. The fact is that he is judging both the Union and the Confederacy, and this judgement, more than any other factor, dictates his selection of dramatic characters, his choice of heroes; in this way, it molds the dramatic action that unfolds before us. One need only compare *To the Finland Station* with *Patriotic Gore* to see how rigid Wilson has become. Where the choice of dramatic actors and thinkers in his study of Marxism leaves even the hostile critic with little to argue about other than interpretation, the reader of *Patriotic Gore* is made to feel that he has been the victim of Wilson's own "moral fanaticism." The abolitionists are condemned without a hearing, or, perhaps worse, with the kind of brief hearing which dismisses them wholesale; they reflect little more than "the capacity for self-delusion of the Bible-drugged New England idealist." The figure who—even if he is not the chief reason for the war's having been fought—haunts the American landscape through the agony of his unresolved presence is all but ignored. So intent is Wilson on dismissing Negro slavery as "the rabble-rousing moral issue which is necessary in every modern war to make the conflict appear as a melodrama" that he virtually blinds himself to the presence of the Negro. The extent to which he himself has been seized by something unfortunately similar to what he once criticized as "Marxist snow-blindness" can be seen if one, in true Wilsonian fashion, checks the book's index. In a volume of some 816 pages, there are three references to Queen Victoria, none to Denmark Vesey; George Washington is cited eight times, Martha Washington twice, Booker T. Washington once. There are eight references to the scholar, Arlin Turner, as opposed to two references to the Negro insurrectionist, Nat Turner (who is dismissed, in one of these, as a "religious fanatic"—similar, no doubt, to his white counterpart, John Brown). Most shocking of all, there is no mention of either Frederick Douglas or W. E. B. Du Bois, each of whom authored autobiographies which shall live in the literature of the Civil War long after Thomas Nelson Page has been justly relegated to the position of a mere footnote in the literary history of the United States.

The Negro is not quite real to Wilson in this book. He concludes his chapter entitled "Diversity of Opinion in the South" with the suicide of Hinton Rowan Helper, then adds, apparently to drive the message home, the following paragraph:

> To such mental and moral confusion were the thinkers of the South reduced by their efforts to deal rationally with the presence among them of four million kidnapped and enslaved Africans of a different color of skin and on a different cultural level from their own.

But it is only in relation to the Southerner and to the agony of the war that the Negro interests Wilson. In a very long book, he never once chooses to look at the slaves as a distinct and relatively homogenous group with a culture, however dessicated by slavery, of their own. He does not bring to the study of the Negro in the South that lively and sympathetic interest which he brought to Zuñi, to Haiti, to the Iroquois. The one black writer with whom he deals is the diarist, Charlotte Forten, who is so strikingly unrepresentative of the slave experience that there are moments when her diary appears to be the work of a Southern belle with a dark skin. Could not Wilson have done better with Du Bois, with Douglass, with Booker T. Washington, or even with Father Henson whose story served as the model for Uncle Tom? Perhaps Wilson found the Negro the most disturbing element in his sea-slug thesis. For if the black man, like the white man, is a sea slug, then can we not expect that a book published in 1962 should have reflected the growing appetite of the black sea slug, an admission that he was no longer content to feed on other black sea slugs?

Since reason for such qualification is obvious, one should make clear that it is not necessary to insist that Wilson place the Negro at the center of American experience, not even at the center of that experience during the Civil War. To do so would be historically indefensible. But does not Wilson, in his desire to do justice to the South, create a picture of slavery which is at best inaccurate and at worst unreal? Not that he does not see the evils of slavery; it is simply that he seems to accept, at face value, such claims as that made by the South Carolinian, Basil Gildersleeve, to the effect that the Southern states were engaged in a war for "the cause of civil liberty and not the cause of human slavery." It is difficult to imagine a more flagrant example of "the capacity for self-delusion" than such a declamation, and the fact that such statements were employed with increasing frequency when it became evident, in the war's later phases, that the South was going to be defeated simply makes Wilson's approval of it more difficult to understand. One wonders whether Wilson's eulogy of Alexander Stephens, who is, with the possible exception of Holmes, the chief figure in his pantheon of heroes—a eulogy which possesses all the passionate conviction and visionary catharsis of which Wilson is capable as a writer—is not his own deeply sentimental eulogy for "the death of the old political South," a country in which the presence of slavery has somehow never quite registered on his mind. One suspects that Stephen's insistence that the South was not a conquered nation, his refusal to recognize the Fourteenth and Fifteenth Amendments, has been absorbed into a moral atmosphere which, in others, produced attitudes far less praiseworthy—the hysterical worship of that collective delusion called the "War Between the States," the lynchings, the suspicion of ideas, the inability to accept change, and the romantic blanket which has, until recently, covered a system which rested neither upon the "cause of liberty" nor the creation of a culture but upon the systematic exploitation, degradation, and dehumanization of one group of men by another. Human slavery looms over American history like that gigantic shadow at the end of Poe's *Narrative of A Gordon Pym* and it should, one guesses, have seized the imagination of a writer who has written what more than one critic called an "epic" of our Civil War.

Nor does Wilson's desire to destroy the mythology of the war excuse his intellectual negligence: he seems curiously oblivious to those myths which do not comfortably fit into his picture of the "aggressive" North strangling the "family" of the South (it is a strange kind of family that keeps more than one third of its members in bondage). His views on Reconstruction, for example, could have been voiced by any one of the twelve contributors to that memorial of the unreconstructed South, *I'll Take My Stand*. But *I'll Take My Stand* was published in 1931, at a time when Wilson himself was impatient with the sentimental Jeffersonianism of its contributors. The Wilson who wrote *Patriotic Gore* sees Reconstruction as a period of "ignominies and errors," a time of extreme "federal repression," which demonstrated, like the imprisonment of Jefferson Davis, "the vindictive animosity of the North." Had the book been written twenty years earlier, one could understand the blanket endorsement of the standard view of Reconstruction. But all during the 1950s, at the very same time that

Wilson was working on *Patriotic Gore,* a significant group of historians had been looking at both slavery and Reconstruction without the prejudices of their predecessors. That slavery would have somehow withered away and died a natural death (a view Wilson seems to endorse) had been effectively questioned by Kenneth Stamp and Stanley Elkins, whose work was available to Wilson long before he completed his study of the Civil War. He seems oblivious to the work of C. Vann Woodward, Eric McKitrick, and John Hope Franklin. And he is far too willing to accept at face value the statements of Southern diarists, such as Mary Chestnut, "that slavery had become to the Southerners a handicap and a burden." The truth is that Reconstruction governments, with all of their many liabilities, were neither as corrupt nor as ineffective as they have been depicted in the past, and that, on such matters as education and civil rights and land reform, they were far superior to the plantation aristocracy which had ruled the South through the Civil War or the bourbon racists who were to take power after the Reconstruction governments had been destroyed. It may be that the tragedy of Reconstruction was not the North's "despotism," that it was, instead, the failure of a political party which might have rescued this nation from what now seems to lie before it, a racial crisis of unprecedented dimensions, had it not traded in its principles for a mess of electoral college pottage.

To argue that the creation of myth gives one the privilege of standing outside history in one's very effort to embrace history is highly dubious. But this, it seems, describes the only way in which many of Wilson's theses in this book can be defended. His indictment of the United States ultimately comes down to the charge that it has cast aside its older republican virtues, the virtues one finds in Herndon's *Life of Lincoln* and in Alexander Stephen's *A Constitutional View of the Late War Between the States,* and has replaced these virtues with power alone through the creation of a political state so immense, so powerful, and so antithetical to the pre–

Civil War dream that it could no longer be considered a suitable home for a civilized man. *Patriotic Gore* is a eulogy for the Republic, a book of lamentations by a prophet who now feels "that this country, whether or not I continue to live in it, is no longer any place for me."

And yet, it is a eulogy which distorts and a vision that is, on closer inspection, somewhat hazy. Our America is, in many respects, a far more troubled country than the country about which Wilson wrote in the book which followed *Patriotic Gore–The Cold War and the Income Tax.* Of one thing we can be certain, however, and that is that it is a different country from the one Wilson describes. For he measures it from the vantage of a myth that may be aesthetically pleasing but is historically distorting. To claim that the jailing of Jefferson Davis "suggests Stalinist Russia" is not merely to voice a rather far-fetched analogy; it is to create a fundamental distortion. Even if we grant that the treatment of Davis and his family was brutal, it is simply not the issue that should have concerned the puritan moralist. For purposes of the kind of myth Wilson is here engaged in creating, the issue should have been the very one that he virtually ignores, Negro slavery. The question of why the North fought the war is not as important as Wilson makes it, atlhough it is true that it was chiefly concerned with preserving the Union. But it is the brutalizing inhumanity of Negro slavery to which one must return again and again. And it is that inhumanity which is so conspicuously absent from this book; it is that inhumanity which today threatens this nation because it has never really tried to come to terms with what it represents; it is that inhumanity which makes Mrs. Howe's "Battle Hymn of the Republic" a far more inspiring song, despite Wilson's sardonic interlinear comments, than "Maryland, My Maryland"; and it is one's recognition of that inhumanity that pulls one up short when he reads a sentence such as this:

There are moments when one may wonder today—as one's living becomes more and more hampered by the exactions of centralized beauracracies of both the state and federal authorities—whether it may not be true, as Stephens said, that the cause of the South is the cause of us all.

The structure of *Patriotic Gore*, unlike the structure of *To the Finland Station*, leaves as much to be desired as its theses. Far too much of the text is made up of long quotations. There are moments when, in going through the book, one feels that perhaps one-third of the text is made up of quotations. Not even the fact that much of the material Wilson here uses is out-of-print justifies such extensive extracts. In order, for instance, to support his claim that Sidney Lanier's work is hampered by his excessive German romanticism (a claim that is fairly obvious to anyone who has ever waded through even a fraction of Lanier's work), Wilson quotes almost three solid pages of incredible slush. Not only is *Patriotic Gore* ill-proportioned, it is also puffy, perhaps because of Wilson's excessive personal consciousness of the period about which he wished to write. And the book's development has not been wholly thought out. The movement from Northern myth to Northern soldiers is followed by a movement which goes from representatives of the Old South to the Southern myth. A chapter devoted to three Confederate women, Kate Stone, Sarah Morgan, and Mary Chestnut is followed by a chapter devoted to three Southern soldiers, Richard Taylor, John S. Mosby, and Robert E. Lee. Wilson then examines Southern thinkers and Southern politicians before he turns to "The Myth of the Old South," a myth which he wished to demolish, although his attack on it is more restrained than his attack on the Northern myth.[4]

In the second half of the book, Wilson turns from the war's participants to the literature that came out of the war, the poetry of Lanier and Whitman (he devotes far more attention to Lanier than to Whitman) and of a number of minor poets, along with the fiction of Tourgee, Cable, Kate Chopin, Thomas Nelson Page, and Ambrose Bierce. Among the best written of all these essays, the one on Bierce contains a summation of what Wilson saw as absent from American writing of the post–Civil War era:

> But there was something besides the crudeness that hobbled his exceptional talents—an impasse, a numbness, a void, as if some psychological short circuit had blown out an emotional fuse.

But these are the most disappointing chapters in the book. They serve best not in the role for which they were intended but as unsatisfactory contrasts for that most vivid of all portraits in *Patriotic Gore,* the concluding chapter on Holmes. Like the book's structure, the prose does not match the prose of *To the Finland Station,* not even in the chapters devoted to Lincoln or to Stephens or even to Holmes. There is nothing to equal the memorable metaphor of Prometheus and Lucifer which gives the portrait of Marx its fine edges and which dominates not merely our image of Marx but our ideas about the evolution of the system which he brought into being as it is developed by the historical actors of *To the Finland Station.* There are even occasional lapses in which Wilson's own prose seems caught up by that very romanticism he criticizes; he describes photographs included in an edition of Lanier's poetry as "burning-eyed strong-willed young girls who spurred on the young men in the Civil War, who flashed their fierce gaze at the Yankees." And he is pedestrian enough to describe the qualities which Grant and Lincoln brought to American prose as their ability to "hit the nails on the head."

And yet, after one has written all of this, after one has noted how Wilson has not sustained us in our need for a new myth, the book remains, almost in spite of its weaknesses and in defiance of our needs, a personal testament to how one can endure history. One need not go back to "The Old Stone House" to understand how deeply personal Wilson's relationship to the historical past has always been. Evidence enough can be found in "The Author at Sixty," even when he rather casually mentions that his father was also named Edmund Wilson. From its very origins, his work had sought the fusion of self and society. After his disillusionment with Marxism, that quest took the form of reentering the world of his father. Just as Proust exonerated his life through the creative act of bringing *Remembrance of Things Past* into being, so Wilson has sought to understand his own life through re-creating—at the very time it becomes foreign to our lives and our country—the world of his father and of Justice Holmes. When one puts this book down, he is aware, above all else, of the terrible price Americans have been forced to pay in order to possess their country, a country which, year by year, recedes from our grasp. Not the least of Wilson's achievements, certainly, was the way in which he re-created the immense bitterness of his father's generation as its members fell before the democratic rapacity, as they revolted, however ineffectually, against the sheer magnitude of self-righteous power and wealth.

What one ultimately values in *Patriotic Gore* is Wilson's own struggle for a sense of continuity which he can bequeath the reader. That Wilson is aware that the country and its culture is at one of those crossroads from which there can be no turning back was evident from *The Cold War and the Income Tax*, a book which, however naïve, seems to have represented a kind of personal clearing of the air. One indicts Wilson for his lack of interest in the contemporary and then one remembers the superlative chapter in *Patriotic Gore* on the virtually forgotton Calvin Stowe. Is there another writer in this country capable of making such a figure seem so immediate? Is there another writer who can make nineteenth-century hypochondria and idealism so vividly relevant? Is there another writer who, searching for heroes with almost as great a fervor as Mailer combing the underbrush of our terror and fear in order to uncover some model of meaningful escape, can bring Grant and Sherman to the kind of recognizable life that we see here? And is there another writer who has endowed Lincoln with a greater sense of believable messianism—and this in spite of Wilson's belief that Lincoln was wrong in his desire to hold the Union together?

The finest of all of these portraits is that of Holmes, with which Wilson chose to conclude his *Studies in the Literature of the American Civil War*. It is not only that Holmes's life and thought crystallize the spirit that Wilson has traced down so relentlessly in this book, that "the young Holmes's experience of the Civil War, besides settling for him the problem of faith, also cured him, and cured him for life, of apocalpytic social illusions." It is that in Holmes Wilson obviously sees himself. The power of the chapter on Holmes is the most personal of all these chapters, and the reader is increasingly aware, as he goes through it, of the at times irresistible desire to substitute the name Wilson for the name Holmes. When one reads, "that he had managed to survive his regiment has become for him a source of pride," one cannot help but sense that Wilson is here writing about his own powers of survival, calling the role of friends dead, of talents decayed, with the knowledge that he, like Holmes, had come through. Even Holmes's relationship to intellectual Jews reminds one of Wilson's own, just as Holmes's desire to reject all myth and to remain loyal to rational analysis seems to be Wilson's ultimate word not merely on the Civil War but on a subject with which he had flirted since he first felt the attraction of Marxism. The ability to stand alone, to remain loyal, finally, not to a conception of the world but to a conception of one's own integrity, one's own striving for the fruition of excellence, this, too, is as characteristic of Wilson as it is of Holmes. In their backgrounds, in their environments, in the intellectual resiliency and the emotional toughness that each of them attained in the struggle with a tradition which, at one and the same time, succored them even while it threatened to choke them, the two men are remarkably similar. When Wilson asks, "How was it that he managed to survive, to function as a first-rate intellect, to escape the *democratic erosion?*" (italics mine) one understands that he is speaking about his own position within this America as much as he is speaking about the position of Justice Holmes. For like Holmes, he sees himself as "a man of the old America"; and like Holmes, too, he can, at this point, claim for himself "the prestige of longevity."

Had *Patriotic Gore* been as successful as a whole as it was in some of its parts, it would have served our culture far better than any number of essays on Genet or the Theater of the Absurd. That it does not altogether succeed cannot alter the conception that stands behind it, where the historian and critic set out to create an idea of a culture and a country. Wilson's refusal to serve the contemporary is not to be regretted; his apparent inability to recognize what is happening in contemporary life is. It is this, certainly, which one discovers in the "protest" with which Wilson, in 1963, announced his momentary return to the kind of problems which had troubled him in the thirties. He remains a model of integrity and he embodies, both personally and intellectually, those very qualities which he celebrated in Holmes. He is a child of the Republic—and this is both his strength and his limitation. For his tendency to simplify, once evident only in his treatment of certain literary figures, has grown to the point where his political writing reflects an attitude that one would be tempted to call naïve were he not writing about Edmund Wilson. That the man who was, in the 1930s, among the most perceptive social critics in the United States should publish *The Cold War and the Income Tax* is simply depressing.

It is not that one argues with Wilson's thesis in the book. But where he had once given an acute, perceptive, and sensitive dissection of depression America, he now sounds, despite the lucidity of his style and the clarity of his sentences, like a crotchety old man who has just discovered that napalm burns children and that our taxes pay for its production. It is here, rather than in his refusal to write about modern American authors, that Wilson seems to have deserted us. For it is here that he should have accepted a position of leadership in the American intellectual community. That celebrated moral force which sent him to Holmes, to Lincoln, and to his own father is something that we need more than ever in this plasticized America. But all that *The Cold War and the Income Tax* does is to make us wonder exactly where Wilson has been since the end of the Second World War. To ignore the present as a literary critic is one thing; to ignore a world that is burning beneath our feet and then to discover the burning with a sense of outrage is quite another. In addressing himself to the question of what our tax money is used for, Wilson discovers the growth of chemical and biological warfare; but his tone is difficult to understand. He writes as if the American public were ignorant of their existence, when the real horror of contemporary America is that virtually no one, not even school children, is oblivious to the uses to which our tax money is put. We accept these revelations as we accept the presence of the bomb—we live in a kind of moral schizophrenia. But we live, and it is this fact upon which we focus.

One does not need to argue with Wilson's diagnosis (although it is rather hurried and not wholly free from his prejudices) or with his conclusions in which he takes his spiritual leave of the country. The argument against the book is an argument against an excess of the personal. For the remedy to our problems, as far as intellectuals are concerned, still lies in our recognition of the necesity of changing the world, even if we are aware that the task is so much more difficult than nineteenth-century thinkers, including both Marx and Holmes, conceived. And there is, finally, something altogether too passive, too complacent, in the sight of one of our great men, perhaps our greatest literary figure, simply deciding that "this country, whether or not I continue to live in it, is no longer any place for me." Of all people, the puritan least of all can claim the privilege of serving when and where he finds it convenient. The difficulty with *The Cold War and the Income Tax* is that it never opens avenues of resistance for us, as, for example, a figure such as A. J. Muste did.

O Canada, put together from articles that Wilson wrote for the *New Yorker* in 1964 and published as a book the following year, is the weakest of all his cultural surveys, chiefly because he seems rather unclear of his purpose. He begins by exploring Canadian literature, another unexplored country; but he soon veers off into the French-Canadian independence movement. As politics has come to have less and less meaning for him, it also seems to have become a kind of analogical catchall. In *O Canada* he repeats his analogy between the fate of the Confederacy and the fate of Hungary. But the fact that each was overrun by a stronger, more centralized, power does not make the analogy particularly pertinent or valid.

O Canada is not very convincing, neither in its literary criticism nor in the connection it tries to draw between the French-Canadian revolutionaries and colonial liberation movements. And Wilson appears to be endorsing a nationalism that is provincial and terribly destructive to that very independence of spirit which he has upheld at a certain personal cost throughout his life. The spectacle of different language groups staking out their exclusive cultural provincialisms in a kind of endless linguistic Zionism does not seem to bother him. On a number of occasions, Wilson has indicted American professors, particularly professors of American literature, for being far too specialized. This would seem to have been a justifiable indictment. But one wonders whether the corollary of this is to see culture in such starkly anthropological terms, the very temptation he was able to avoid in *Red, Black, Blond and Olive*. And one wonders whether those meddlesome beaureaucrats who have stirred his anger and wrath are to be feared as much as those who, in the name of self-determination, are ready to destroy God if they cannot get him to change his face. There remains something to be said for an ideal of culture which is international. More than anything else one can think of, Wilson's own writing exemplifies this.

5

Survival

The world cared little for decency. What it wanted, it did not know; probably a system that would work, and men who could work it; but it found neither.

From *The Education of Henry Adams*

In one of the few truly dispassionate articles written about Edmund Wilson, Frank Kermode paid him his highest possible tribute when he noted that Wilson had worked at "the legitimate and exhausting tasks of criticism . . . as no other critic in his time." This is a far greater tribute to Wilson than either the presidential Medal of Freedom, awarded him in 1963, or the Gold Medal for Essays and Criticism which he received from the American Academy of Arts and Letters in 1955. For Kermode's recognition is the recognition of a peer, the kind of statement with which Wilson himself could be pleased. To have done one's work, and to have done it in the face of the shoddy, the meretricious, and the hysterical—all of which have swamped so many other American writers in our century and swept them under—is to have fought actively for that very integrity which had always been his goal.

And yet, as we have seen, he has paid for his professionalism and integrity, and the price has been far greater than the culture which now institutionalizes him is ready to admit. How painful is the monumental probing of the country in *Patriotic Gore*. Wilson may not be, as he wrote of himself, living in the eighteenth century, but he is certainly the last of a vanishing species. One is almost tempted to call him the last American. And he is, above all, the American as a man of letters. The kind of self-exile which he has chosen for his old age finds its equivalent not only in the New Englanders, Jews, and Southerners who have occupied so much of his attention during the past two decades of his life, but in the artist's decision to pursue his vision, of Joyce wandering through Europe, of Proust in his cork-lined room, of his friend, Fitzgerald, staving off the end in the graying protoplasm tissued between streaks of Hollywood neon. In these comparisons, one can see the extent to which Wilson has been a product of his times, another child of the first half of the century who strode onto the intellectual stage equipped with both a sense of self and a sense of shared destiny.

For if Wilson is, as Frank Kermode also writes, "the greatest periodical critic of his time," it is apparent to other critics that he wanted a different achievement than the one fate has granted him. Proust and Joyce were as much his models as Mencken and Croly, and one finds, even in his early work, traces of a desire to create a public self capable of absorbing, like some sensitive barometer, what Hazlitt meant by the "spirit of the age." Wilson has frequently been compared to Emerson, a comparison first made, apparently, by F. O. Matthiessen in the thirties. And one should not forget that Emerson was speaking of this, too, when he conceived of his representative man. This simply adds greater irony to the image Wilson has finally succeeded in creating, that of the writer as patrician—and an increasingly distant patrician at that. As Wilson moves further and further away from the center of American life, his intellectual intransigence, like his insistence on the enduring validity of the world from which he stems, has come to seem an irritant, at the very same moment we recognize that he has, through preserving these qualities, succeeded in making an indelible mark on the national consciousness.

Having served, in Alfred Kazin's phrase, as "the conscience of two literary generations," Wilson has been, almost unnoticeably, metamorphosed into the father of a third and a fourth. But it is one of the fates of fathers, especially in America, that they come under attack by their sons. In part, this may be dismissed as one of the inevitable aspects of literary success in America. Wilson had endured, and endurance itself has now become, as we whip ourselves into a frenzy of praise for the irrational, a decidedly suspect attribute in our America. But if this alone were the substance of the charges against him by the younger American critics, that he has, again in Richard Gilman's words, "become increasingly detached from the central life of culture in this country, a life he once helped shape and color," then one could simply dismiss the charges as an example of those personality wars all too frequently fought on a literary battlefield. But the charges go much deeper and they possess a certain validity. For when one examines the work Wilson has done since the publication of *To the Finland Station* in 1940, one finds that he has been guilty of creating his world at the expense of our reality. His magnificent loyalty to a conception of self that embodies both integrity and excellence has been matched, unfortunatly, by a shrinking sense of human involvement and by an apparent withering away of his own sympathies.

One sees this is not only in *Europe Without Baedeker*; one sees it, too, in the crotchety conservativism of *The Cold War and the Income Tax* which focuses upon "property" like some aging James Fenimore Cooper. That the power to tax is the power to destroy is a rather tiresome axiom; it is also the power to create and one wishes that Wilson could now show greater concern for the kind of suffering to which he gave such eloquent testimony in *The American Jitters*. But this is the very quality which is absent from *The Cold War and the Income Tax*, which is why the book is not, as Sherman Paul calls it, "an example of the kind of gesture open to intellectuals" in our time.

To see how enclosed Wilson has become, one need only compare him—not, as he so often is compared, to the New Critics, those aging warriors who have been flayed for so long that their flesh is not only scarred but their doctrine is no longer recognizable—to Camus, or, better still, to Orwell. If dignity is among the hallmarks of the permanent, one must admit that Orwell reserved, in however ultimately paranoid a manner, the better fate for himself. Far more personally bitter than Wilson, far more pessimistic about the fate of civilization in our century, Orwell still managed to remain at the center of the resistance until the moment of his death. Perhaps this is not altogether fair to Wilson, since Orwell died in 1950 at the age of forty-seven. But to anyone familiar with his work, it is virtually impossible to think of Orwell in the role of old curmudgeon, increasingly alienated and increasingly honored by the formal culture. To the very end, Orwell remained bitterly loyal to possibility. At the time when Wilson began his retreat from the center of contemporary life, Orwell was dissecting a world in which the technologists of modern civilization were flying overhead trying to kill him. The essays which he produced during the war are fed by the deepest springs of honesty and are stamped with the humanity of a contemporary. For this reason, Orwell, like Camus, has become a model for those younger intellectuals who believe that his world is old-fashioned, that the possibilities of which he conceives are not wholly plausible, but that he himself remains a model for the intellectual's participation in the things of this world. And if one compares the work they were doing in the thirties, it is easy to see how close to one another Wilson and Orwell were, how each was enmeshed in trying to strike out against that common inhumanity which had produced the common suffering.

In the beginning of this book, I mentioned that I was nineteen when I first read *The Shores of Light.* As I read it, I could feel myself being seized by an immediacy and excitement which few other books—certainly no other collection of journalistic reviewing—were to give me.

Part of this is to be attributed to Wilson's idea of what criticism was. For Wilson was telling me, in these collected weekly reviews and essays, that a culture was that which endowed life with its proportions and that a critic was an individual whose taste and intelligence served to illuminate those proportions and to make them available. Perhaps his greatest virtue, from my point of view, was his ability to share his sense of discovery, to communicate without even trying why literature was important. He was never to be successful at creating a theory of literature, and his attempts to do this, like *The Wound and the Bow*, are not very convincing as theory. And yet, where a critic such as Kenneth Burke heightens our sense of critical methodology, Wilson heightens our awareness of the writer in his world. Perhaps it is preferable to be offered access to the writer's world than to be offered a critical structure imposed upon that world. Theories of literary criticism tend to use the artist's imagination to the point at which they must discard it. Wilson, on the other hand, has always been concerned with the centrality of imagination, both as a critic and as a writer of dramatic history.

My experience with Wilson seems to me worth mentioning only because it also seems to me representative. During the years in which I was a graduate student of literature in America, where scholarship is an industry and where Joyce is a product, Wilson served me as he served so many of my peers: he kept our love of literature alive. So much of what one was forced to read was the product of a lack of imaginative vitality coming into contact with imaginative vitality, the work of men who seemed to have little passion and less empathy for literature. Wilson was a living example of the possibilities of intellect in America, the very embodiment of what the creative intelligence could achieve. He was so markedly different from the kind of men who, in the years ahead, will undoubtedly subject Shakespeare to the computer.[1]

And yet, at that very time, he had already taken his leave of us. He was to remain an intellectual and he was never to subscribe to any of the "smelly little orthodoxies," allegiance to which Orwell saw as so characteristic of intellectuals. Increasingly, however, he was to become a victim of his own endurance.

Wilson's particular fusion of intelligence and lucidity is rare in any literature, at any period of time. One suspects that the ability to produce such a fusion may finally be what we mean by the word *culture.* His passion for literature, his intellectual curiosity, his ability to penetrate to the core of a problem without stranding himself somewhere on its peripheries—such qualities have made him a permanent part of the American's cultural legacy. And they help explain the source of our younger critics' disappointment in him. For Wilson is still read eagerly. One must take into account what he is saying at any particular moment. The trouble is that he now rarely says very much of significance to us. Still, we continue to read him, because we expect so much. We read him when he appears embarrassing and even naïve, as he is in *The Cold War and the Income Tax;* we read him as he scours the recesses of a past that means far more to him than he is able to give to us; we read him when, ignoring the advice of Trotsky, he conceives of history as a plot and of politics as hopelessly corrupt; we read him when he returns to a Europe in which, we know, he could never have truly felt at home and complains like some native of Keokuk whining for ice water on the table. We read him, finally, because he demands, as only the finest of writers can demand, that we come to some kind of very personal terms with what he has to tell us. In this, he is the closest thing we have to a major nineteenth-century novelist. He is the product of his world; the source of *Patriotic Gore* may ultimately rest in the *New England Primer.*

Had Wilson written nothing more than *Axel's Castle* and *To the Finland Station,* he would be able to claim for himself a preeminent position in our literature. Like it or not, he has been our Emerson—even when the times demanded a Thoreau. Having given us an example of the kind of integrity which our world finds both frightening and meaningful, he has the right to move wherever he wishes. We, on the other hand, have the right to be disappointed in Wilson's withdrawal from the issues which plague us. But who can deny that he has done his work well? And what more can one demand of fathers than that they represent continuity—especially in our time of fragmentation?

Notes

3—The Retreat from Politics

1. But it should be said that where Wilson understood the centrality of class, Orwell thrust himself into a class other than his own, impelled by a terrible and deeply rooted guilt as well as by his courage and compassion. The differences between how the two men thought about class can probably be attributed to the conception each of them held of the middle class. For Wilson, the middle class was derived from the world of his father; he saw it as professional, as striving for excellence, and as accepting the necessity of responding to the world at the very same time that it was pessimistic about the prospects of meaningful change. Orwell, on the other hand, had the world of the small tradesman in mind when he wrote about the middle class. George Dowling of *Coming up for Air* is his prototype. *Down and Out in Paris and London* is Orwell's attempt to reach bottom, to purge himself of all former class attitudes. Not even *The American Jitters* approaches it in this respect. Regardless of how deep his sympathy for the oppressed is or of how great his anger at the oppression is, Wilson knows that he is a journalist, who is, in a manner of speaking, passing through. He does not sentimentalize the "common life" in *The American Jitters,* as to some extent he did in his two excursions into fiction.

2. There are a few unfortunate exceptions to this, such as the description of a brunette as "rather pretty but not quite first-rate." For a writer who has so vehemently insisted on precision in the use of language, Wilson is occasionally

given to such stale expressions. Richard Gilman has pointed out how, in his criticism, Wilson has sometimes been guilty of the use of these expressions to the degree that they become "ludicrous, such as in his reference to a 'first-rate saint.' " On the whole, however, Wilson is certainly among the better stylists in American literary history, to the extent that when he does err it is far more noticeable than it would be in another writer. In *Memoirs of Hecate County,* his writing falls down in its didacticism. Perhaps because it is so autobiographical, he had even more difficulty in keeping the critic and journalist at a proper distance in writing this book than in writing *I Thought of Daisy.* What is so striking about the book's autobiographical roots is that Wilson was now trying to capture both the world of his father and the world with which the book treats.

3. The chief impressions the reader receives from Wilson's 1963–64 diary of his European stay are of his physical discomfort and spiritual irritation. De Gaulle's Paris is plagued by an "atmosphere of official repression"; its women lack "chic," its monuments have lost their "glamor," and its people are in the process of destroying French "culture." Rome is "more open and cheerful than Paris," but half of the twenty-eight pages devoted to it treat Punch-and-Judy shows, which Wilson does not manage to make as intriguing to the reader as they obviously are to him. The pages devoted to modern Rome, as a matter of fact, show us one of the very few times when Wilson did not communicate a vivid physical sense of the city he is visiting. The one city that appears to have captured his imagination on this trip to Europe was Budapest, which he was seeing for the first time and about which he seems genuinely curious. But his *Diary* is a rather flimsy affair, apparently added to the original book to give it some new selling point. Strangely enough, despite Wilson's growing distrust of the United States, which he speaks about in the preface to the new edition of *Europe Without Baedeker* and which had already manifested itself in *Patriotic Gore* and *The Cold War and the Income Tax,* America remains the measuring rod. "Though they rail at us, they have envied and idealized us."

4. To an unfortunate extent, criticism of Wilson's work has constituted rival polemics about what the function of criticism is. This is as true for Wilson's adherents as it is for his detractors. (The terms themselves suggest that Wilson has become a kind of critical battlefield.) The chapter which Hyman devoted to Wilson in *The Armed Vision,* a chapter which he subsequently deleted from the paperback version of the book, is curiously personal. It offers an indictment of Wilson virtually en masse, and it distorts, perhaps deliberately, many of Wilson's attitudes. On the other hand, to attribute Wilson's "almost total neglect in the schools" to this chapter, as Sherman Paul does in *Edmund Wilson: A Study of Literary Vocation in Our Time,* seems highly questionable. Hyman is unfair and personal, but if the schools have neglected Wilson—and this is itself questionable—it is because of his conception of critical responsibility, the lucidity of his prose, and his sometimes irritating antiacademicism. Judging by the recent exchange in the *New York Review of Books,* Wilson believes that the Modern Language Association *is* academia. It might even be suggested that one could make a fairly good case about how Wilson has neglected the schools, where his debts may be greater than he has admitted. The whole question of Wilson's reputation is dealt with by F. W. Dupee, himself a judicious critic and brilliant teacher, in a long review of the reissued *Europe Without Baedeker* that appeared in the *New York Review of Books.* Like Frank Kermode, Dupee attempts to see Wilson clearly and to see him whole, and while he praises Wilson generously he also descries the tendency to elevate Wilson's "Reputation" at the expense of other critics and of literary criticism itself. Wilson's reputation has, of course, always been raised or lowered by the prevailing literary winds. When textual analysis dominated our English departments, Wilson's reputation suffered a serious decline. But in the fifties, when the limitations of textual analysis began to make themselves apparent and when a kind of cultural nativism seized some English departments, his reputation once again began to climb. Now that socially conscious criticism is once again as natural as mother's milk, Wilson seems to be in danger of

being relegated to the position of a grand old man, the literary equivalent of Norman Thomas.

4—Home as Found

1. It should be noted that this essay, originally published in the *New Yorker* on October 19, 1957, was reprinted in an expanded version as the prefatory essay to David Magarshack's translation of *Turgenev's Literary Reminiscences* one year later. But a number of the other essays included in *The Bit Between My Teeth* had also previously been published more than once.

2. Wilson's usual method of work is to review books which touch upon interests that he himself is working on. As early as 1928, he had written a fascinating review contrasting the chief characters in two biographical studies, John Charles Fremont, the pre–Civil War American explorer, and Henry Clay Frick, the post–Civil War steel magnate. Fremont and Frick are dramatically pitted against one another in this review: both are, in their ways, "giants," but where Fremont still belongs to an America in which heroic possibilities are as wide as the geographic horizons, Frick is one of "the performers of a colossal rogues' comedy." The review concludes with a sentence that hints of Wilson's emerging Marxism: "And what new kind of American in what new field may our country now be ready to breed to provide us with heroes and leaders?" But of the figures who were to make up *Patriotic Gore,* only George W. Cable appears in his work during the twenties, when he reviews a life of Cable written by his daughter. The first review-essay incorporated into *Patriotic Gore* was "Francis Grierson: Log Cabin and Salon," which appeared in the *New Yorker* on September 18, 1948. On November 27, 1948, an essay on Harriet Beecher Stowe's *Uncle Tom's Cabin* entitled " 'No! No! No! My Soul Ain't Yours, Mas'r!' " was published in that same magazine. For the next eleven years, at least half of the review–essays Wilson wrote were devoted to books about or by figures he was to include in his Civil War gallery.

3. One wonders what Wilson's reaction is to the changes taking place within the Catholic Church today. His anti-

Catholicism is rather similar to his anglophobia. It is only fair to point out that if the liberalizing tendencies within the Church are successful, then the Church which he personifies in *The Little Blue Light* as the Children of Peter will no longer resemble the Church Wilson attacked. In the play, the character who is Wilson's intellectual spokesman compares the Children of Peter to the Communists: "Actually the objectives of the Peters are just about the same as the Reds', and their methods are about the same. The only difference is that they're directed from Madrid [the Vatican], not Belgrade [the Kremlim] and that they make use of a different mythology. Their principal instruments are father confessors instead of third-degree police. But both the Reds and the Children of Peter want to get rid of education and to keep the working class down."

4. From Robert Penn Warren's *The Legacy of the Civil War*, published one year before *Patriotic Gore*, Wilson took the phrases *Treasury of Virtue* and *Great Alibi* to describe the ways in which the North and the South had deluded themselves about the war.

5—*Survival*

1. As I type the final copy of this manuscript, I discover in the *New York Review of Books* that Shakespeare has already been subjected to the computer. According to the reviewer, he survived.

Selected Bibliography

In a bibliography of Edmund Wilson's work compiled by Arthur Mizener for the *Princeton University Library Chronicle* of February 1944, items are included which go back to Wilson's contributions to the *Hill School Record* in 1910. And Wilson has been, for almost sixty years, a professional writer who has not only written well but has written a great deal. Professor Mizener's "Checklist" is invaluable, but it is, of course, limited to the work Wilson did through 1943. Since that time, much of Wilson's earlier work has been republished in new collections and much of it has been revised. For the most part, these revisions have been stylistic, although there have also been substantive changes in some of the republished work. And, of course, the material with which a republished work is included makes a great deal of difference in the way we look at it. Not only was the Russian section of *Travels in Two Democracies* reprinted with previously suppressed materials twenty years after its original publication, it was also incorporated into his study of Zuñi, Haitian, and Israeli cultures, where before it had contrasted with his observations on the United States during the first two years of the New Deal. The same can be said of *The American Jitters,* which is a far more powerful book when read by itself than when read as part of *The American Earthquake,* where it was reprinted minus "The Independent Farmer" and "The Case of the Author." All I have attempted to do here is to list Wilson's books in chronological order, as well as to note the present availability of his work.

1922 *The Undertaker's Garland,* in collaboration with John Peale Bishop. New York: Alfred A. Knopf.

1926 *Discordant Encounters: Plays and Dialogues.* New York:Albert & Charles Boni. The material in this book was subsequently included in *The Shores of Light, A Piece of My Mind,* and *Five Plays.*

1929 *I Thought of Daisy.* New York: Charles Scribner's Sons. Republished by Ballantine Books in 1953; again republished, along with the short story, "Galahad," by Farrar, Straus & Giroux in 1967.

1929 *Poets, Farewell!* New York: Charles Scribner's Sons. Most of the material in this volume was reprinted in *Night Thoughts.*

1931 *Axel's Castle: A Study in the Imaginative Literature of 1870 to 1930.* New York: Charles Scribner's Sons.

1932 *The American Jitters: A Year of the Slump.* New York: Charles Scribner's Sons. Reprinted in *The American Earthquake,* except for "The Independent Farmer" and "The Case of the Author."

1936 *Travels in Two Democracies.* New York: Harcourt, Brace and Co. The American portion was reprinted in *The American Earthquake,* along with some additional material, and the Russian portion was reprinted in *Red, Black, Blond and Olive,* along with some material Wilson had originally suppressed. The prologue, flashback, and epilogue of the original were omitted from these later editions.

1937 *This Room and This Gin and These Sandwiches: Three Plays.* New York: New Republic. Reprinted in *Five Plays.*

1938 *The Triple Thinkers: Ten Essays on Literature.* New York: Harcourt, Brace and Co. Revised and enlarged in 1948.

1940 *To the Finland Station: A Study in the Writing and Acting of History.* New York: Harcourt, Brace and Co. Reprinted with different appendixes as a Doubleday and Co. Anchor Book.

1941 *The Boys in the Back Room: Notes on California Novelists*. San Francisco: Colt Press. Reprinted in *Classics and Commercials*.

1941 *The Wound and the Bow: Seven Studies in Literature*. Boston: Houghton Mifflin Co.

1942 *Note-Books of Night*. San Francisco: Colt Press. Most of the material in this volume was reprinted in *Night Thoughts*.

1943 *The Shock of Recognition: The Development of Literature in the United States Recorded by the Men Who Made It*. Garden City, N. Y.: Doubleday, Doran and Co.

1946 *Memoirs of Hecate County*. Garden City, N. Y.: Doubleday, Doran and Co. Reprinted in 1959.

1947 *Europe Without Baedeker: Sketches Among the Ruins of Italy, Greece, and England*. Garden City, N. Y.: Doubleday and Co. Reprinted together with *Notes From A European Diary: 1963–64* in 1966.

1950 *The Little Blue Light: A Play in Three Acts*. New York: Farrar, Straus and Co. Reprinted in *Five Plays*.

1950 *Classics and Commercials: A Literary Chronicle of the Forties*. New York: Farrar, Straus and Co.

1952 *The Shores of Light: A Literary Chronicle of the Twenties and Thirties*. New York: Farrar, Straus and Young.

1954 *Eight Essays*. Garden City, N. Y.: Doubleday and Co.

1954 *Five Plays*. New York: Farrar, Straus and Young.

1955 *The Scrolls from the Dead Sea*. New York: Oxford University Press.

1956 *Red, Black, Blond and Olive: Studies in Four Civilizations: Zuñi, Haiti, Soviet Russia, Israel*. New York: Oxford University Press.

1956 *A Piece of My Mind: Reflections at Sixty*. New York: Farrar, Straus and Cudahy.

1956 *A Literary Chronicle: 1920–1950*. Garden City, N. Y.: Doubleday and Co.

1958 *The American Earthquake: A Documentary of the Twenties and Thirties*. Garden City, N. Y.: Doubleday and Co.

1960 *Apologies to the Iroquois*, with *The Mohawks in High Steel* by Joseph Mitchell. New York: Farrar, Straus and Cudahy.

1961 *Night Thoughts*. New York: Farrar, Straus and Cudahy.

1962 *Patriotic Gore: Studies in the Literature of the American Civil War*. New York: Oxford University Press.

1963 *The Cold War and the Income Tax: A Protest*. New York: Farrar, Straus and Co.

1965 *O Canada: An American's Notes on Canadian Culture*. New York: Farrar, Straus & Giroux.

1965 *The Bit Between My Teeth: A Literary Chronicle of 1950–1965*. New York: Farrar, Straus & Giroux.

1967 *A Prelude: Landscapes, Characters and Conversations from the Earlier Years of My Life*. New York: Farrar, Straus & Giroux.

Index